Sunset

Deepest silence everywhere,

The sun sets.

No branch is moving anywhere,

And I walk alone,

Lonely as always.

There's no love anywhere.

My heart rejoices

   when I weep

And my sorrows gain voices.

Gods! Just let me have this!

Wilhelm Lehmbruck, 1902

The Art of Wilhelm Lehmbruck

Reinhold Heller

National Gallery of Art
Washington

Distributed by
The Macmillan Company,
New York, New York
Collier-Macmillan Ltd., London

The Macmillan Company
866 Third Avenue, New York, N.Y. 10022
Collier-Macmillan Canada Ltd., Toronto, Ontario

Library of Congress
Catalog Card Number: 72–76727
First Printing
Printed in the United States of America

contents

Preface and Acknowledgments   6

Foreword   8

Author's Acknowledgments   10

Introduction   11

Catalog   35

Lenders to the Exhibition   37

Plates   63

Color Plates   65

Sculpture   73

Paintings   124

Drawings and Pastels   130

Etchings   158

Lithographs   176

Appendices   179

Biographical Notes   180

Exhibitions 1906–1918   182

Exhibitions 1919–1971   183

Bibliography   186

preface and acknowledgments

The exhibition signalized in this volume represents the first major exposure in America of Wilhelm Lehmbruck's artistic achievement since an exhibition in 1930 when the Museum of Modern Art in New York included eight of his works in a small exhibition, "Lehmbruck-Maillol." In the present show, paintings and graphics as well as sculpture are displayed in a single exhibition for the first time in the United States.

It would not have been possible to carry out this project without the full cooperation of the Republic of Germany, the City of Duisburg, and the Lehmbruck Museum, for these are national treasures cherished and preserved by the artist's home city and his family. Our very special thanks go to Guido and Manfred Lehmbruck, the artist's sons, for it is they who have immeasurably lightened the task of preparing the exhibition and the catalog by supplying both practical assistance and unlimited access to their extensive family archives.

In addition, we have obtained loans from several institutions and private owners for whose generosity we are deeply grateful.

We are very pleased to have been able to secure as author Professor Reinhold Heller of the University of Pittsburgh. His studies of 19th and 20th-century European art have made him particularly qualified for his research in the art of Wilhelm Lehmbruck. Many insights into Lehmbruck's chronology and style appear in this volume for the first time, and we hope it will contribute to a literature in English on the artist which has been surprisingly insubstantial. Professor Heller has collaborated with the Lehmbruck Mu-

seum in Duisburg in the selection of works included in the exhibition, and has conferred extensively with colleagues in Germany as well as with the Lehmbruck family in preparing this catalog.

Douglas Lewis, Curator of Sculpture at the National Gallery of Art, was the curator in charge of the entire enterprise, and thanks are due him for his splendid work. Thanks are due also to Moussa Domit, formerly of the staff of the National Gallery of Art and now Associate Director of the North Carolina Museum of Art in Raleigh, whose assiduous attention to the details of preparing this exhibition has been fundamental to its realization. Mr. Domit was assisted by the photographer Walter Klein of Düsseldorf who produced all but a very few of the photographs for this catalog.

After its showing in Washington, the exhibition will travel to the University of California at Los Angeles, the San Francisco Museum of Art and the Museum of Fine Arts, Boston. We are grateful for the collaboration of these institutions in the project. Thus audiences on both coasts will be able to benefit from a wider and more detailed review than has heretofore been possible of Lehmbruck's accomplishment as an artist, an assessment of what he produced in his short working life and what has been done since to put into enduring form his images and dreams. I feel confident that this opportunity for a new study of his works will confirm his rank as one of the principal masters of the early 20th century.

J. Carter Brown
Director

6

I believe we are again approaching
a truly great art and that soon we
shall give expression to our time through
a monumental contemporary style.
It must be of our own time,
not a reacceptance of
older styles, for none of the
great epochs of past art was founded
on the resurrection of styles from
previous centuries. The style
must be monumental, heroic, like
the spirit of our own time.

Sculpture, like all art,
is the greatest expression
of our time.

Wilhelm Lehmbruck

foreword

Wilhelm Lehmbruck is one of the few German sculptors of the 20th century whose stature as an artist has met with appreciation and acceptance.

Lehmbruck's first major exhibition was at the Galérie Levesque, Paris, which opened only a few weeks before the outbreak of World War I. It brought together such key pieces of his as the *Kneeling Woman*, and *Pensive Woman*. Wilhelm Lehmbruck took part in the epochal 1913 Armory Show in New York which was the first comprehensive exhibition of contemporary European art ever to be shown in the United States. In it Lehmbruck was represented by his *Standing Female Figure*. The American collector Stephen C. Clark purchased the piece and later gave a bronze version of it to the Museum of Modern Art in New York. This gift, together with the Armory Show (which took place more than half a century ago), marked the beginning of Lehmbruck's acceptance in America as an important contemporary artist. Two decades later the Museum of Modern Art mounted its exhibition "Maillol and Lehmbruck" and the critical and public acclaim which greeted it clearly reflected the genuine enthusiasm for Lehmbruck's sculpture in the United States.

Following the Second World War, the artist's sculpture was honored by extensive exhibitions throughout Europe. A museum named after him was erected in his native city of Duisburg, thus providing a permanent home for his entire oeuvre. The architectural design was created by his son, Manfred Lehmbruck.

The Wilhelm Lehmbruck Museum is situated in a park within the city center and consists of two heterogeneous structures which enclose an open-air sculpture garden. The wing housing the oeuvre of Wilhelm Lehmbruck is a spatial analogy to his work, making visible (in his son's words) the "fusion of art and structure" where "the exposed concrete expresses things lasting, final and timeless." In contrast to the "static calm" of the museum stands the "dynamic character" of the other section: a glass-sheathed, transparent hall, constructed through means of a suspension system. This section runs parallel to a main thoroughfare of Duisburg. With its flexible interior the building fulfills the "requirement of variation and improvisation."

It houses a 20th-century sculpture collection with an international flavor, including works by Brancusi, Lipschitz, Laurens, Gabo, Giacometti, Pevsner and many others. Here, too, relevant temporary exhibition can be installed, and again, to quote the museum's architect, "the spatial arrangements can be changed to suit the exhibition material." The entire building, in plan and elevation, has at its core a unifying module. With this artistic concept, the son followed his father, the ingenious sculptor Wilhelm Lehmbruck, whose words, cast in lead, greet the visitor at the museum entrance: "All Art is Measure".

Siegfried Salzmann
Director, Wilhelm Lehmbruck Museum
Duisburg

Every work of art must retain something from the first days of creation, something of the smell of earth, or one could even say: something animate. All art is measure. Measure seen against measure, that is all. The modules, or in figures the proportions, determine the line, the silhouette and all else. Therefore, a good sculpture must be handled like a good composition, like an architectural edifice, where measure speaks against measure; therefore, details cannot be ignored, for the detail is the module for greatness. The painter who subdivides the surface does the same as the sculptor who sees the expanse of his statue as a surface and subdivides it. Therefore, no monumental, architectonic art exists without an outline or without a silhouette, and a silhouette is nothing more than flatness. Filled with intensity, nothing bare!—filled with warmth, filled with depth! Among a few young artists from the most varied countries I have discovered this common feeling, although their works all appear quite different from each other, and this feeling shall lead them to a new expression for our time: to the style of our time. Sculpture is the essence of things, the essence of nature, that which is eternally human.   *Wilhelm Lehmbruck*

author's acknowledgments

The task of compiling the catalog and its documentation would have been impossible without the generous support and cooperation of the sculptor's son, Mr. Guido Lehmbruck, who diligently guided my study of the family archives and patiently answered numerous questions. Similarly, the Wilhelm Lehmbruck Museum, Duisburg, kindly permitted the investigation of its own unequaled collection and the use of its research facilities; the entire staff of the Museum deserves my utmost thanks, but I particularly wish to single out its director, Dr. Siegfried Salzmann, and its curator, Dr. Tilman Osterwold, both of whom gave much of their time in aiding my studies. The bibliography would not have become such a major addition to Lehmbruck research without Miss Margareta Kroczek, who sifted through German periodical listings and library holdings to provide a preliminary listing of writings on Lehmbruck. For their enthusiastic support during some of the more trying moments of the exhibition preparation, I wish to thank particularly Douglas Lewis and Grose Evans of the National Gallery of Art, as well as Moussa Domit, now Associate Director of the North Carolina Museum of Art, who joined in making the initial exhibition selection.

The staff of the Fine Arts Library at the University of Pittsburgh should be mentioned for their aid in finding books and articles as I needed them, and for putting the bibliography into its final state. I am also indebted to Frances Smyth, Assistant Editor of the National Gallery, who guided the catalog through its various stages from manuscript to final copy.

A special note of appreciation and thanks must go to my wife Vivian. Without her patience, support and encouraging impatience, as well as her typing skills, I probably would still not have completed the catalog. Also to be remembered are my students at the University of Pittsburgh who have engaged in informative discussions with me concerning Lehmbruck and modern sculpture; they in turn have benefited from the invaluable training I received through my teacher, Professor Albert Elsen, who first encouraged my interest in Lehmbruck.

Reinhold Heller

Introduction

Wilhelm Lehmbruck was thirty-eight years old when he committed suicide in 1919. At a time when he had attained public acclaim and success and the major museums of Germany were purchasing his sculpture, he deliberately ended his life, convinced that the future possessed no values for which he could live. The first war of the twentieth century had taken place, had destroyed promises of human brotherhood, had elevated murder above art, had created hatred, hunger and distrust, and a world of revolutions and civil wars was not the world for his intensely quiet, contemplative work. The war and its diseases had killed other artists—Franz Marc, Raymond Duchamp-Villon, Egon Schiele, Gustav Klimt, Umberto Boccioni, August Macke—and it had turned him, a German, into the unwilling enemy of Fernand Léger, Alexander Archipenko, George Minne, Auguste Rodin, Amadeo Modigliani and others whose art he admired and who were his friends. For Lehmbruck, only his own death could erase these errors of fate, and his death became a supplication for peace and a sacrificial self-immolation in a world which had declared war on art. His death was also the suicide of an artist filled with self-doubt, uncertain of himself, intensely melancholy and easily depressed, unsure of the future of his art and therefore willing abruptly to end its development.

Paul Westheim, Lehmbruck's biographer, wrote: "Lehmbruck's work remains a torso. . . . He has given us much that is significant, but, judging from his beginnings, we had the right to expect more, greater perfection, greater universality."[1] The unfulfilled search for perfection and universality which Westheim attributed to Lehmbruck was an inherent part of the development of German art during the nineteenth century and the initial decades of this century. Not since the sixteenth century had Germany been an essential component of the European art world. As in the Scandinavian countries and England, most of German art was a reflection, often belated, of French or Italian or Netherlandish artistic currents and its greatest significance was on a local rather than European scale. In part this may have been caused by a lack of national identification or purpose in a Germany splintered into hundreds of independent states and cities, each jealous of the other. During the *Sturm und Drang* and romantic movements at the end of the eighteenth century, the concept of a Pan-German identity and the idea of a German nation were revived and intensified into a proud nationalism during the wars against the Napoleonic Empire. In their attempts to establish a consciousness of Germany as a national concept, German artists played a major role, placing their art at the service of national pride as they sought to establish a national content and style whose quality would equal or even surpass the quality of French art.

Novalis, the German romantic poet, prophesied in *Christianity or Europe* (1799) that a new spirit was being born in Germany free of worldly imperfections. "We can already recognize with certainty the traces of a new world in Germany. Slowly but surely, Germany proceeds in advance of the other European countries. While others occupy themselves with wars, speculation and party strife, Germans are busy transforming themselves into members of a new, great cultural epoch, and their precedent will in time certainly give them a definite advantage over the other countries. In the sciences and the arts there is great activity. The spirit is being immensely developed. From new, fresh sources, creation is taking place." The German artist was to cease seeking his models and masters in Italy or France, but was to find them in his own past, in the cathedrals of the Middle Ages and the paintings of Albrecht Dürer. In returning to his national origins he would guarantee the originality and quality of his art. "As our ancestors acted and believed in naïve innocence so should we believe and act from experienced knowledge," wrote the painter Caspar David Friedrich.[2]

The goal of the nineteenth century was to create once again a national German art, to return German art to the realms of international significance which France appeared to monopolize. Within this goal was contained an antithesis. The artist who concentrated on the national identification of his art, most notably in content, could not communicate with a non-German audience, whereas the artist seeking to attach himself to international formal developments quickly found himself neglecting the national qualities of his work, setting abstract artistic ideals above all other values. Numerous German painters and sculptors attempted to combine the two goals to form a synthesis of German and Roman or Parisian ideals, of intensely felt content and supra-national formal vocabulary. Among these artists is Wilhelm Lehmbruck. It is this duality of intention which in turn contributed to his uncertainty, which increased the difficulty of fulfilling his task, and which made the intra-European animosity such a desperate situation for him.

Lehmbruck received the training common to sculptors of the last century. In his schooling nothing separated him from numerous other skillful artists later to be forgotten, and yet in his training lay the foundations and principles which determined the character of Lehmbruck's later sculpture. In the summer of 1895, at 14, Lehmbruck entered the School of Arts and Crafts in Düsseldorf, a school designed to teach the crafts of all the arts in preparation for specialization in the Academy. Lehmbruck had already been drawn to sculpture as a craft and had carved small plaster figures based on statues he found illustrated in his schoolbooks. Probably to fulfill the requirements of his school, he created a small self-portrait in plaster in 1898, depicting himself stiffly in a realistically conceived portrait bust of a style popular during the late nineteenth century [1]. * It is an initial attempt at capturing in three dimensions something of his own character, but is largely a student work practicing the basic skills of sculpture, a demonstration piece for his teachers and intended to meet their criteria.

Working within such a firm set of criteria also characterizes Lehmbruck's activity at the Düsseldorf Academy where, as a student, he came under the influence of Karl Janssen. Janssen (1855–1927), a highly successful sculptor, and an Academy professor since 1893, had obtained numerous commissions for public monuments in the city, mostly fountain figures and memorials to German political heroes. He thus set for his students, including Lehmbruck, the major example of contemporary greatness, the most significant living sculptor in a city rich in artistic tradition. Janssen devoted much time to the creation of religious sculpture as well—statues for churches and grave monuments —for German and American patrons. He was one of the first German sculptors to reflect the stylistic and ideological influence of the Belgian sculptor Constantin Meunier.

In Germany at the turn of the century, the name of Meunier constituted a sculptural program. His work had been known there since the early 1890s and in 1896 had entered the prestigious collection of the National Gallery, Berlin; at the same time, he continuously exhibited with the less traditional Secessionist movements in Munich, Berlin and Vienna. Meunier's figures of workers and miners depicted at times of rest, concentration or sorrow, in a highly idealized, classicizing realism, appear as sculptural monuments to the heroes of modern technological society, and indeed as new Christ-like martyrs to industrial progress.

*Numbers in square brackets refer to pieces in the exhibition.

Using the style of traditional nineteenth-century sculpture, Meunier contributed a new subject matter to modern sculpture. It was this combination of conservative formal vocabulary with radical content into a sculptural declaration of the worker's dignity that appealed to Karl Janssen and other artists in the Rhine and Ruhr industrial complex of Germany. In Meunier they discovered the means of communicating the radical ideals of the workers and their dominant political party, the Social Democrats.

The theme of Courbet's *Stonebreakers*, with a mother and child replacing the man and boy of that painting, was taken up by Janssen in 1902 while Lehmbruck was his student. The work received immediate critical acclaim. Janssen presents a young mother, perhaps even a young widow, who pauses briefly in her stonebreaking work to gaze at the baby resting at her side. A dual sense of pathos is set up; on the one hand the viewer is intended to feel a sense of sympathy or perhaps even indignation at the sight of the poorly clothed yet noble woman forced to work at this menial task to support her child; and secondly, the viewer should recognize the bond of love passing between mother and child as their eyes meet, and therefore respond with a sense of compassion. It is a highly literary, sculptural creation whose dual purpose is to present the message of the exploitation of workers by their employers and of the workers' inborn aristocratic spirit unbroken by life's burdens.

Between 1903 and 1905, while still under Janssen's influence, Lehmbruck created several works possessing the same didactic character. One, *Firedamp*, a monument to coal miners killed in a mine explosion (Fig. 1), depicts the body of a miner stretched out on a bier; while his wife

Figure 1

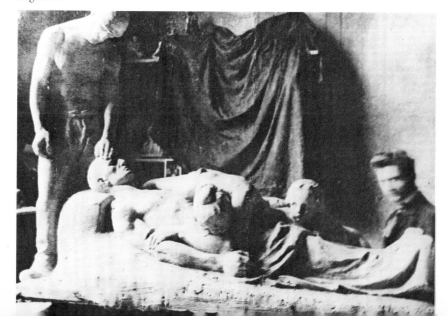

Figure 2

collapses and weeps over the body, in much the same way as traditional representations show Mary Magdalene weeping over the dead Christ. The miner's child stares wildly in total incomprehension, and another miner stands priestlike, his head bowed in noble grief, at the head of the corpse. Also conceived in a monumental and classically idealized style is a project composed of figures of workers for a *Monument to Labor* (c. 1904; Fig. 2), which, like Janssen's sculpture, is closely related to the work of Meunier—who also designed a similar *Monument to Labor*, as had Auguste Rodin and Jules Dalou. Similar in theme to this project are a small statuette of a worker rolling a stone, a muscular model dressed in miner's pants and boots pushing against a massive stone like a new Sisyphus [3], and a relief of a miner, originally bearing the title *After His Labors*, who sits on a rock in a pose related to Rodin's *Thinker*, again wearing the working uniform of a miner and carrying a lamp as if he were a modern Diogenes [4]. They are sculptures conceived on Janssen's didactic example and searching for a synthesis between a traditional formal vocabulary and the content of a society whose conscience had been formed by the writings of Emile Zola and Gerhard Hauptmann. They are also sculptures derived from Lehmbruck's own life as the son of a miner who spent his youth in a mining town. They proclaim Lehmbruck's desire to create sculpture relevant to modern man yet personal in its source, sculpture modern in stylistic conception yet building on the vocabulary of tradition. This new ideal would mark all his works.

The "modern" theme of labor was not, however, Lehmbruck's sole concern during his years as Janssen's student. Specifically academic works as well as sketches for symbolist compositions were conceived at the same time. The motif of the bathing nude, made popular in Germany by the sculptors Reinhold Begas and Max Klinger, appeared in Lehmbruck's sculpture in 1902, shortly after he entered the Düsseldorf Academy.[3] *The Bathing Nude* is again a demonstration piece displaying Lehmbruck's mastery of human anatomy, his ability to treat such illusionistic details as the pressure of the hand on the flesh of the right hip and his solution to the problem of rendering the pliable qualities of a woman's body in the hard material of bronze or plaster [2]. The little figure is an exemplary work in the academic genre, and it earned Lehmbruck a fellowship and a position as "Master Student." All the elements treasured by the academy are present: the female nude illusionistically rendered yet retaining a firm sense of structure, and of the contrapposto play of engaged and relaxed legs and arms. The figure is self-enclosed and provides a smoothly flowing silhouette clearly read despite the bending posture, and yet the harshness of the frontal silhouette is alleviated by the twist in her body which creates a slight turning motion directing the viewer around the sculpture. All the elements of the sculpture can be clearly read from a single frontal view, yet the sculpture contains devices which also cause the viewer to investigate it in terms of its mass and its three-dimensional qualities. This conception of sculpture as a basic silhouette combined with an exploration of mass is dependent on the theories developed by the German sculptor Adolf von Hildebrand in his book *The Problem of Form in Sculpture* (1893), a highly influential study not only in Germany but also in France and the United States, and also serves to characterize Lehmbruck's later sculpture, and forms the basis of his definition of sculpture as "measure against measure."

The academic nude female figure was combined with the mother-child relationship of Janssen's *Woman Breaking Stones* in the first sculpture sent by Lehmbruck to Paris [6]. Sketches for *Mother and Child* (1907) indicate the group was conceived at a time when Lehmbruck was fascinated by the Faust legend, particularly by the tragic figure of Gretchen. Lehmbruck's *Faust* illustrations refer, however, not to Goethe's famous play, but rather to the one by Nikolaus Lenau, whose Faust drama is deeply melancholic, with a protagonist filled with despair and ultimately committing suicide. Perhaps Lehmbruck saw something of his own brooding uncertainty in Lenau's *Faust*, but from initial studies depicting Gretchen's pangs of conscience after she had drowned her illegitimate baby, Lehmbruck arrived at a representation of woman as a life-giving, protective force, as a *mater misericordia* gazing compassionately into the eyes of her newborn child. The creative process of moving from a specific source of inspiration or experience to a related expression of more universal values, a process dependent on the aesthetic values of fin de siècle symbolism, was again applied by Lehmbruck here, as it had been in his depictions of laborers and miners three years earlier. This was the process through which he continued to work.

Figure 3

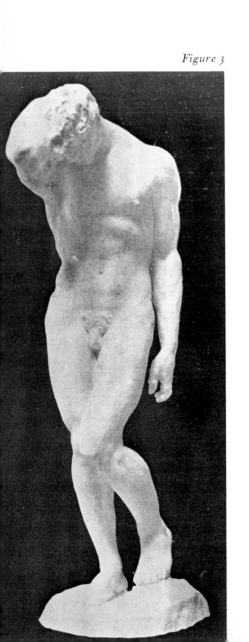

The self-contained formal structure of *Mother and Child*, of a single form enclosing two figures within itself, was repeated in a high-relief variation on the same theme where the mass of the child's head is incorporated into the silhouette of the mother and compositionally replaces the volume of her right breast. Instead of gazing at her sleeping child, the mother has an introverted look of melancholy, a difference of conception also revealed in the title, *Meditation: Mother and Child* [7]. This contemplative pose is shared by several other works from 1907–09, notably *Grieving Woman* [9], another relief in the same tabletlike shape as *Meditation*. Since *Meditation* apparently existed at one time in a marble version, and since Lehmbruck was working on several other grave monument projects at this time, these two works mark a continuing interest in a genre practiced extensively by Janssen even after Lehmbruck had terminated formal connections with the Academy. Many of these pieces originated in connection with Lehmbruck's inclusion in the 1909 Düsseldorf Exhibition of Christian Art and might be seen as little more than means of financial support, as incidental creations, were it not that Lehmbruck's constant, deliberate return to themes of death and grief points to a morbid fascination related to the concerns of the symbolist movement and most notably embodied in Edvard Munch's art.

Sculpture as gestural symbol of emotional states: this was Lehmbruck's credo as an artist, a credo which he developed shortly after leaving the Academy. The Academy, and notably Janssen's example, provided the style with which to clothe this concern. Lehmbruck did not develop an individual style until 1910; the years 1907–1910 show an artist seeking to overcome his academic predilections and leaving the safety of neoclassical form. The language of Rodin was the first employed to accomplish this liberation process. Rodin, whose sculpture Lehmbruck had admired since 1904, embodied the yearning for an art which was of its own time rather than a pale reflection of sculptural glories from the past, and Rodin was also the most successful among those sculptors who had broken with academic traditions. Perhaps inspired by Rodin's *Walking Man* at the Salon of 1907 which he had seen on his first trip to Paris, Lehmbruck adopted Rodin's modeling and heavy, naturalistic form for a monumental ten-foot tall depiction of *Man* (Fig. 3), the most eclectic of all his sculptures, formed by combining diverse elements from Rodin's *Adam* and *Eve* and *Age of Bronze*, as well as the arm and hand of Michelangelo's *David*. This additive process demonstrates how deliberate and conscious was Lehmbruck's rejection of academic formulas. There was not a series of changes but rather a single, unpredicted, total change in everything but content, and Rodin's use of the entire body as a gesturing symbol gave Lehmbruck the means of presenting again a mood of melancholy, indecisive contemplation.

Rodin's successful work was not the only one emulated by Lehmbruck in his attempts to overcome academic tradition; the work of the Belgian symbolist sculptor George Minne is reflected in Lehmbruck's figure of a woman, initially conceived as his entry in a competition for the sculptural decoration of a department store designed by the Jugendstil architect Josef Maria Olbrich (Fig. 4). The nude figure and the contrapposto posture derive from Lehmbruck's academic training, as does the closed formal structure with its strong consciousness of the silhouette's linear value. The academic effect was reduced by the influence of Rodin's active surface texture as it was applied by Lehmbruck in the small bronze statuette created as a variation on the competition sculpture. What is more significant for his later development is the elongation of body forms, notably in the legs, lower torso, and neck-shoulder areas. The extended body form and silhouette emphasis perhaps derive directly from Minne's *Fountain of Kneeling Youths*, purchased in 1902 for the Folkwang Museum in Hagen, a city near Düsseldorf. It is known, at any rate, that even later Lehmbruck retained great admiration for George Minne's melancholy sculptural forms. But the elongated form also recalls the mannerist sculpture of Jean Goujon and the School of Fontainebleau, with which Lehmbruck may have become familiar during his first trip to France. Lehmbruck, however, replaces the delicate sensualism of the mannerist figures with a simplification and reduction of form into a tightly defined architectonic structure more akin to neoclassical sculptural concepts [8].

The uneasy eclecticism of the sculpture created upon leaving the Düsseldorf Academy resulted from Lehmbruck's loss of faith in the value of the academic philosophy that had previously controlled his sculptural vocabulary. There was no longer a single, proven formula to which he could revert, and his resulting self-doubt and the inability to guarantee success is revealed in the attempts to combine elements derived from nonacademic but publicly accepted sculptors such as

Figure 4

Rodin and Minne who were also being imitated by numerous other German sculptors of the time. The academic habit of following a defined pattern remained a crutch to Lehmbruck as he groped for his vision of "a monumental, contemporary style, not a reacceptance of older styles." In Düsseldorf, he lacked the confidence and the model which would have made possible the initiation of his own independent art; Janssen's academic eclecticism could not be totally overcome.

Before the Paris Salon opened on April 15, 1910, Lehmbruck had settled in Paris with his wife and one-year-old son.[4] At the Salon, he exhibited two portrait busts, and his monumental *Man*; all three displayed an extremely close dependence on Rodin. In Paris Lehmbruck also was able to overcome his stylistically derivative and eclectic approach to sculpture by rejecting Rodin's example of dramatically activated surfaces and returning to values ultimately dependent on his academic training. According to reminiscences of Frau Anita Lehmbruck, the imitative adulation of Rodin as a grand sculptural father-image characteristically ended suddenly, following Lehmbruck's visit to Rodin's atelier in Meudon. After seeing Rodin's works collected there and engaging in friendly conversation with the French sculptor, Lehmbruck returned to his own atelier and resumed work on a new sculpture, *The Standing Female Figure*, perhaps originally conceived as a pendant to the *Man* much like Rodin's *Adam* and *Eve*. But in the completed sculpture, the dangerous flirtation with Rodin was totally overcome. By breaking with Rodin, Lehmbruck achieved his first independent work.

Just as Lehmbruck created his Rodinesque *Man* in 1908–09, abruptly and without a series of transitional works leading away from his academic manner, so no bridge of transitional work exists between the *Man* and the *Standing Female Figure*. As the sole reminder of his visit to Rodin's studio, he initiated the practice of creating not only the full figure but also partial figures; the legless, armless torso and the head exist as concentrated statements of the total work. In this single figure, Lehmbruck achieved a precise definition of his relationship to the past as well as to his contemporaries, but now no longer found it necessary to quote from them.

Lehmbruck exhibited a tinted plaster cast of the figure at the Salon d'Automne in October, 1910, in conjunction with his *Mother and Child*

Figure 5

of 1907 and the 1909 grave relief *Grieving Woman* [9], both works still echoing his academic vocabulary. It is as if he wished to indicate a conceptual relationship between these two sculptures and his newest work. In contrast, at the Salon in April, all his works had been Rodinesque in manner and indicated an avowal of faith in Rodin's example as the guide to the creation of new sculpture. By October, this faith was totally denied. As a further definition of his current stylistic sources, he exhibited a large colored drawing, *Frieze of Women* (Fig. 5), which depicted seven nudes in a landscape and used a friezelike organization dependent on his practice in sculpture but also related to the paintings of Hans von Marées, the highly form-conscious German artist who had sought a synthesis of classical form and German thought during the nineteenth century and whose work was exhibited in Paris for the first time in 1910. Using his newly created *Standing Female Figure* [10] as the focal point, in the Salon d'Automne Lehmbruck affirmed his attachment to his German, academic training and to the search for a synthesis of modern German and classical romantic traditions while overtly rejecting the French example of Rodin. The *Standing Female Figure* was a new proclamation of faith in the viability of German art and, seen within the context of the Paris exhibition, in the inherent equality of German and French artistic achievement.

And yet, Paris, with its diversity of stimulation and its atmosphere pulsing with constantly new artistic ideals, was the necessary arena for Lehmbruck to develop sufficient self-confidence to overcome Rodin's tantalizing example, and to evolve a new idiom from his academic training. The figure stands nude except for drapery tied around her legs, and has a contrapposto posture clearly derived from the example of numerous Greek statues of the goddess Venus; but at the same time is not an imitation of them. Using a module in which the body was subdivided into multiples of twenty-five centimeters (which were equal to the height of the head), Lehmbruck turned to a language of tightly

organized architectonic forms, submitting the human body to an ideal-
izing emphasis on the harmonious coexistence of the parts within the
unifying contour provided by the silhouette. It was the first systematic
application of his principle that "All art is measure, measure against
measure, that is all." He rejected all action and anecdotal detail to at-
tain a greater sense of sculptural severity limited in gesture to the
essential definition of the act of standing gracefully in a state of pensive melancholy.

The tendency towards formal simplification and unification is para-
mount. The fullness of the body with its fleshy forms melting softly
into each other, an effect heightened by the nuances of patina Lehmbruck created most notably in his plaster and stone casts to decrease the
optical hardness and coldness of the material, contrasts with an emphasis on line in the smooth movement of the contours. Lehmbruck almost
works against the material in his attempt to transform sculpture into
a spiritual carrier of mood. Line is emphasized, mass is softened, and
the figure rests with an illusion of weightlessness on the narrow juncture
of her ankles.[5] The significance Lehmbruck placed on the creation of a
spiritual quality in his sculpture, as well as its relationship to German
traditions, was indicated in 1915 by Wilhelm Schäfer, who had known
Lehmbruck since his studies in Düsseldorf:

> The *Standing Female Figure* at first glance appears to depict nothing
> more in her posture than, for example, the well-known *Standing
> Man* by Adolf Hildebrand . . . But it is instructive to compare the
> heads of the two sculptures, because then the unique life inherent in
> Lehmbruck's work begins to speak. It is both less of a prototype and
> less of a stylistic exemplar; nature appears rather to have been grasped
> directly, and when we examine the entire form, we can follow this
> closeness to nature, this "modern" intensity to the tips of the fingers
> and toes and we come to realize that the classical pose is solely an
> outer shell to which life has not been sacrificed. It is entirely impossi-
> ble to move in thought from this figure immediately to the Renais-
> sance where Hildebrand's viewpoint rests, but we have a far stronger
> recollection of the innocence apparent in those original [i.e. archaic]
> Greek sculptures which today speak more to us than the "classic"
> admired during Thorvaldsen's time. More youth, more attachment
> to nature is apparent here, and I only hesitate to call it "intimacy"

because that beautiful word has been sadly worn out with sentimentality.[6]

It is this sense of melancholy intimacy, in combination with the blurring effect softening the juxtaposition of body forms in an almost Praxitelean manner, that also distinguishes Lehmbruck's *Figure* from the sculpture of Aristide Maillol, who is usually viewed as the influence replacing Rodin in Lehmbruck's development.

Maillol had been known in Germany since early in the century and had as one of his chief benefactors Harry Graf Kessler at Weimar. He was known chiefly for his small works made to decorate interiors designed by Henry van de Velde, and not for the large figures he had created since 1902. It seems unlikely, therefore, that Lehmbruck knew of Maillol's monumental figures prior to coming to Paris in 1910, and he probably did not see them until the Salon d'Automne where the *Standing Female Figure* was exhibited and where Maillol exhibited his *Pomona* of 1907. Lehmbruck and Maillol reached in the Salon a similarity of formal appearance without direct influence. The content embodied in these forms is, however, quite different. Maillol's women represent a voluptuous and robust ripeness and weighty massiveness. Lehmbruck deprived the sculpture of its weight and created a woman who was pensive and quiet.

The common interest with Maillol appeared solely in this work; Lehmbruck immediately moved away from the formal vocabulary characterizing his most popular and financially most successful work. *Small Female Torso* of 1910/11 [17] already reveals a renewed interest in the elongation of forms first explored in 1908, and this attempt to combine the emphasis on tectonic structure attained in the *Standing Female Figure* with a new sense of proportion was further explored in the *Small Pensive Woman* [19] and in the relief *Temptation* of 1911 [11]. In the *Kneeling Woman* [22] this tendency in Lehmbruck's search for a personal, modern style found its first major expression.

The theme of a kneeling figure was one Lehmbruck had explored previously; in projects at the Academy, later in angels surrounding a sarcophagus, and in 1910 in the engraving *Mother and Child* [93], which reveals the source of the motif in Madonna figures and is rendered in the volumetric manner of the *Standing Female Figure*. Also in this stylistic vocabulary is a drawing of a kneeling woman, probably an initial study for the sculpture. From these works it becomes apparent that Lehmbruck conceived of the *Kneeling Woman* initially as a kneeling version of his large standing figure and that the attenuated dimensions evolved as he worked on the sculpture itself. Lehmbruck worked on it fitfully, hesitatingly, unable to see it finished. It was his wife who decided to have it cast and to register it for exhibition in the October Salon d'Automne. Still uncertain of himself, and often deeply depressed, he took to wandering through the streets of Paris with his young son. It was only after he heard a few words of praise for his new work and discovered that "some think it's good" did he accept the *Kneeling Woman* as his newest creative work.

The reason for his uncertainty must have been the great stylistic change the work represented. How drastic this change in style was for both the artist and his admirers is indicated in a reminiscence written by Julius Meier-Graefe:

> One day all portrait busts, all torsos retaining a reminiscence of the Greek spirit had been moved aside, and in the center of the atelier there stood a huge female creature, half-kneeling, appearing to have no end to her. She contradicted everything in the spirit of Hans von Marées and even more the closed forms of Maillol. At first glance, she looked most like an awkward giant marionette. Lehmbruck asked what I thought of his cast.

> My disappointment knew no bounds. Here was an artist with the unheard-of luck of capturing the composure of antique sculpture, and he gave it up for a single original notion, for a leap into the blue. I had considered him "safe," and my anger over my own error increased my bitterness towards this slitlike phantom. In my anger, I called it Gothic. It cut through the air like a steep reef and forced the viewer to either kneel down or to flee. I chose the latter, but first told him what I thought. What was he doing with this Gothic stuff? This clumsy bit of work could be anything imaginable, but certainly not sculpture. "That's possible," he said. Naturally, I soon came back. . . . It is necessary to see the *Kneeling Woman* more than once to recognize the language of her limbs, of her raised hand growing like a five-stemmed etheral blossom, of the hand resting and breathing on the extension of the leg and of the foot that flees backwards into eternity, and of the language of the humbly bowed head. Certainly

it is a far different reaction than the one we have in front of the *Bust of Frau L* or the *Small Female Torso*, which present themselves as indivisible units. Now we have to examine each part like the face and look of a person when we speak to them, and only after doing this can we discover the unity existing between the parts. Then every form appears different. Breasts, arms, legs, hands previously torn apart and empty gain a calm ripeness. The raised hand continues the dream of the face and even the distant foot is a necessary conclusion derived from the upward thrust of the body. We discover similarities to the *Bust of Frau L* and even to the *Small Female Torso*, a related play of surfaces, but now born from a totally different impulse and brought to service for a totally different expression. Then it is possible to view the antique elements of the *Portrait Bust* as a first step; certainly a smoother surface movement filled with nobility, and the *Small Torso* has the charm of a blossom; marvelous works but comparatively silent for our generation of unrest which has removed itself from antiquity and needs new appearances, if only to make it possible to wither away on some endless path. Then it is possible that the vocabulary of the *Kneeling Woman* shall become a summons, even if we do not know where it is leading us, and that we shall think back to the silence of the earlier works as to a lost world. It is possible, but hopefully it shall not be, for when we leave the silent world of the *Portrait Bust* we leave behind much that is irreplaceable. Apollonian existence flees, frightened away by a beckoning hand.[7]

Meier-Graefe recognized three significant aspects of this sculpture: the lack of reference to stylistic exemplars, the similarity of attitude to earlier Lehmbruck works and the new emphasis on detail.

Reference to previous stylistic eras, even the reminiscence of the antique, is totally lacking; whatever Lehmbruck's stylistic sources were, they are not openly revealed, but transformed into a unique personal vocabulary which could not be predicted. It was for this reason that Meier-Graefe's reaction was so drastic, until he studied the *Kneeling Woman* sufficiently to find the connections with Lehmbruck's earlier work.

Ernst Barlach, reflecting on Lehmbruck's work, at one time commented: "I simply found it unsculptural and had to reject it. But as a drawing, I would have accepted it."[8] A reaction analagous to Meier-

Graefe's, it also points to the significance of sculpture not as a space-engulfing or space-rejecting heavy mass, such as Barlach's sculpture, but rather as a lyrically moving silhouette outlining a spiritualized kneeling figure. The *Kneeling Woman* is conceived essentially in accordance with Adolf von Hildebrand's concepts of synthesizing in sculpture a two-dimensional form that reveals itself in three dimensions. The architectonic transformation of nature manifests itself in a precise ordering of parts within the enframing line defining content; the human body is transformed into a type of "ideal architecture" related to the functional mysticism of Gothic cathedrals. This stylizing approach to the human form is revealed most clearly from a view of the figure's right profile in which a series of parallel motions, beginning in the inclined head and then reappearing in the raised arm, the line of the drapery and the supporting leg, subdivides the figure and breaks up its mass; but at the same time movements are inaugurated which indicate depth, and thus act against the silhouette's two-dimensional appearance. Minor views are thereby introduced to reveal further aspects of the work, and to increase the total conception of the main silhouette as counterpoint acts on a melody. The meaning of the sculpture is then contained not only in the full revelation of the figure, but individual elements or fragments likewise contain the meaning *in nuce*. The bust of the *Kneeling Woman* could be isolated by Lehmbruck as a concentrated variation on the melancholy, contemplative, ethereal existence of the full figure. As Lehmbruck said, "The detail is the module for greatness."

The elongation and attenuation of forms which appeared in the *Kneeling Woman* became characteristic of Lehmbruck's work and was to be his stylistic signature. It was a device, always combined with strong consciousness of line, found quite often in works by other European artists of the time. Picasso's "Blue Period" paintings, Modigliani's portraits, Kokoschka's and Schiele's drawings and Brancusi's *Prayer* come to mind most easily, but Lehmbruck's *Kneeling Woman* also seems to retain recollections of Minne's *Youths* and perhaps even of Munch's *Madonna*. All were concerned less with finding in the human figure a sense of massive weight, and more with revealing the soul hidden by the material appearance of the human body. This process of sublimation and purification speaks to the viewer in a tone of quiet reverence, giving rise to a feeling which would, as Munch described it, cause him to take his hat off as if he were in a church. Within this context, and recalling the *Kneeling Woman's* origins in the kneeling Madonna, Lehmbruck's sculpture serves as a new religious art clothed in a new iconography of subjective emotion and contemplation, an art and an iconography such as German artists had been seeking for more than a hundred years.

The German poet Theodor Däubler, the subject of a lithographic portrait by Lehmbruck, wrote:

> In sculpture, an ethical verticality must appear once again. Fantasy must once more stretch itself upward; frightened moods should flee out of themselves. A great soul can, however, only appear in a great style, for the soul spills over and scatters, but at the same time loves the form from which it may emanate. We are speaking of Wilhelm Lehmbruck. His *Kneeling Woman* is the preface to expressionism in sculpture. Here we no longer find prayer but rather devotion, a faith in the verticality yet to come . . . Lehmbruck's *Rising Youth* has become the trigonometric viewpoint of sculpture. A masterly touch has subdivided his legs so that a human body can become architectural. Modern self-contemplation accompanied again by a steep, conscientious, upward, structural thrust.[9]

The *Rising Youth* [27], begun in 1913 but not exhibited until 1916, intensifies the structural effects of the *Kneeling Woman*, as Däubler indicated. The profile emphasis of the 1911 sculpture is, however, subordinated to a strong sense of frontality, a reflection of trecento Italian painting or of the Egyptian sculpture Lehmbruck admired at this time. The movement implied in the title is rejected by the sculpture itself as the figure stands on one straight, spindly leg and the other leg props up the torso in a manner often compared to a Gothic flying buttress. The youth is stiff, almost iconlike and is cut sharply from the surrounding space as he engages in an egocentric I-Thou conversational relationship.

A comparison of the head of the *Rising Youth* and Lehmbruck's own face reveals that the artist had created a self-portrait, as he would in all male figures made after this. If one takes into account that after 1909, the sole portraits by Lehmbruck are of his wife or of someone closely related to him (such as the Falk family who were his major patrons, or writers like Fritz von Unruh whose plays he greatly admired) and that his female figures from 1910 until 1917 all bear the features of Frau Lehmbruck, then all Lehmbruck's sculptures can be seen as veiled self-portraits. The apparent objectivity of his portraits thus forms but another aspect of his subjective, autobiographic approach to art in which all sculptural structures become carriers of his own mood projections. It is a subjective approach shared with the painters of the expressionist movement as well as with Ernst Barlach, and is again closely dependent on the German tradition of art developed in romanticism, which viewed all images as reflections of the artist's inner life.

The relationship to expressionism is best seen in Lehmbruck's paintings. The themes—nudes, sexual scenes, pietàs—are shared with the sculpture and prints, but the technique appears to differ, having greater emphasis on facture and the retention of marks of the artist's hand, all characteristics akin to a Rodinesque approach to sculpture rather than to the relatively smooth surfaces of Lehmbruck's sculpture between 1910 and 1917. The painting *Susanna* [58], included in the 1913 exhibition at the Galerie Levesque in Paris, can serve as a basic example. The motif is biblical, again reflecting a preference for themes having academic approval, themes possessing a proven tradition but personally conceived and often possessing symbolic connotations. The overall tone of the painting is sombre; dark blues, greens and browns are applied in quick, slashing brushstrokes and often leave large areas of the canvas free—painting techniques ultimately analagous to the patina achieved in his sculpture. The manner of paint application with the thinned paint being absorbed by the canvas or dripping freely on its surface, as well as the compositions limited to a few figures psychologically related to each other and hierarchically situated, is dependent on the example of Edvard Munch, although it is difficult to determine a precise time of initial influence.

Lehmbruck conceived of his paintings as equal to his sculpture and often exhibited them together, along with prints and finished drawings. The paintings, like the prints, form an addendum to his sculptural work, capturing motifs of multiple figure arrangement for whose sculptural execution he lacked the material means. Themes already explored in sculpture could find further expression here, as the *Kneeling Woman* does in the later painting of a *Crouching Female Nude* [62] or the print *Medea* [114]. Or themes were treated whose subject matter made them unsuitable for the monumental scale of sculpture, usually scenes of sexual violence and death: abductions, crucifixions, floods.

The violent and sexual content of the paintings and prints as well as their manner of execution bring them within the sphere of figurative expressionist painting as practiced by the artists of *Die Brücke* in Dresden and Berlin, as well as by the artists associated with Herwarth Walden's *Sturm* gallery and periodical. With the important exception of Ludwig Meidner, however, Lehmbruck had little to do with these artists and his art is significantly different from theirs. At all times he seeks to give an indication of the plastic qualities inherent in the human body and to order these within a structural framework, rather than immerse them in a total submission to expressionist pathos which appears to reject overtly conscious control.

The desire to submit the forms of nature to his control, to bring order to the seeming chaos of his life experiences, is apparent in all of Lehmbruck's work. The *Pensive Woman* of 1913/14 [31] is a slender, attenuated structure growing in terms of defined intervals until she attains the delicate form of her slightly inclined head. Torso and head could be viewed as separate but harmonizing structural units, again clearly defined by a space-excluding silhouette and the modulating subdivision of the body, each a distinct form organically related to the total structure.

The dependence of his sculpture on his own state of mind permitted the works in Paris, from 1910 to 1914, to be intensely melancholy yet quiet. The *Pensive Woman* seems confidently to dream her own existence. This sense of calm, of having attained independence from the limitations of matter, and of having gained repose in spiritual knowledge ended when World War I broke out. A time of restlessness began for Lehmbruck and resulted finally in absolute despair. His art took on the altered mood. He created drawings and prints treating the motif of fallen, wounded, dying women and men, representatives of the sacrifices of war. In 1916, the *Fallen Man* [45] was exhibited. Paul Westheim, on leave from the front, described the sculpture:

A fallen youth is depicted, cramped in his collapsed position. 'Dying Warrior' is written on a label, perhaps put there to inform the exhibition public; perhaps Lehmbruck also thought of something like this because of the stump of a sword clamped in the youth's right hand. Whichever way it may be, what we see is a young warrior who somehow, in the force of a charge or in the heat of hand-to-hand battle, received that little piece of lead which has torn him down. But this is a death which the body is resisting. The body, which may after all deny its own weaknesses and at such a moment need have no memory of the metaphysics of self-sacrifice, the body reacts and accuses, and screams, and refuses to accept the fact of its end. The head, beating down between the shoulder blades like fire slung from the cannon, bores into the ground in despairing helplessness, as if protection could be found from the death being spewed forth that day. Likewise the hand, that one hand which claws at the earth as if it wanted to take a piece of this world, on which suddenly it will no longer exist, along into eternity. A grasping motion which is not enraged but also not tender, just as we have heard that a dying child reaches out with its last efforts for the mother's breast. One of those incomprehensible gestures which are so irrational and yet so true. And next to this resistance, this stiff barrier against a blind fate, there is the tender elegy of the other hand which tentatively reaches out so far into uncertainty. A weapon, a tool of death now becomes useless, drops from this hand. Reconciliation with what has happened, transfiguration or something of this sort seems to appear. From this furthest extension, Death the Redeemer seems to be entering the body given to him. And yet there is no reconciliation, no appeasement in this work. Something burdensome, something of the anxiety of creation as it learned that the great Pan was dead, is the mood emitted by this figure. For once again a world has collapsed, a world filled with love, filled with activity, filled with happiness, a world whose focal point had been this hero. There are no soft lines, no melting surfaces in this body. Even in the form there is groaning and grating and oppression.[10]

Such a contemporary description testifies to the power of the *Fallen Man* to treat the essential loneliness and hopelessness of the war experience, and reveals Lehmbruck's ability to transform this into a formal structure abstracted from the human form. In this sculpture and in the *Seated Youth* [48], begun at this time and completed in 1917, Lehmbruck's translation of the human organism into an independent sculptural creation reaches an extreme never again attained by him.

In both figures the body consists of a series of hard, geometric surfaces into which the tubular structures of the limbs project. As never before, Lehmbruck uses the entire form to define expressive voids, around which the figure appears almost like a silhouette. The sculpture itself approaches an existence as line encircling a sculptured space; the figure becomes a tightly encircling receptacle of its own spatial actions in the intense dramas of grief or death. This expressive interaction of volume and void, as well as the rigid submission of nature to the transformations of artistic structure, are concerns shared by Lehmbruck with the artists of Paris, notably Alexander Archipenko and cubist sculptors such as Jacques Lipschitz, who at this time were resorting to the device of placing holes within their sculptures to show a solid-void interaction. It is as though Lehmbruck had moved the concerns of Parisian art to Berlin and symbolically incorporated them into a statement not only on the general agonies of war but specifically on his shattered hopes for a new international style of art. As in the drawings and prints he created in Berlin while seeking to escape the oppressive atmosphere of war, Lehmbruck's *Fallen Man* is a dying genius and the *Seated Youth* is the despairing artist.

In these two works, Lehmbruck completed the transformation of his academic training into a modern sculptural vocabulary; but the milieu and artistic dogma that had made this transformation possible were in Paris. Lehmbruck in Berlin was deprived of the support needed to continue the exploration of his personal synthesis of tradition and innovation of Germany and Europe. Deprived of an international artistic circle having similar concerns, Lehmbruck was forced to escape into himself and there search for further inspiration. His introspective personality turned increasingly to a repetition of deeply depressed states. He seemed to be grasping for a lost world of security, and an illusion of it appeared in the neutrality of Switzerland. But the Zurich in which dadaism was being born provided no true haven for Lehmbruck's desire to give tradition a modern form.

In style his sculpture returned to a fascination with Rodinesque surface drama, and only figure fragments were created. A small *Female Torso* [51] appears almost like a figure from Rodin's *Gates of Hell* in its emphasis on surface manipulation and excited action; only the elongation of the figure recalls works Lehmbruck created immediately prior to it. Perhaps Rodin's death in 1917 inspired a return to the example Lehmbruck had followed only briefly previously. *The Thinker* [53] again takes up Rodin's motif but removes from it the muscular activity of Rodin's *Penseur* and transforms thought into a brooding battle indicated by the lumpy surfaces of the brow and the fist clenched on the chest. Details are in danger of overpowering the sense of total organization and structure previously emphasized, but at the same time a vocabulary has been developed in which gestures of strong emotional and psychologically dramatic content have been reduced to an intense minimum. *The Thinker* consists solely of a head raging vertically on the strongly elongated neck from the horizontal of the shoulderline, and of a single hand clasped against the modulating planes of the chest; all else has been eliminated as superfluous.

Similar expressionistic reductions of forms, with harsh contrasts appearing between smooth surfaces and violently active ones, characterize all works from the last year of Lehmbruck's life. He returned to themes derived from his studies at the Düsseldorf Academy, notably the mother and child. Perhaps inspired by the birth of his third son, Lehmbruck worked on the mother and child relationship both in graphics and in sculpture. The prints concentrate more on the coexistence of mother and child as a formal problem, whereas the sculpture melts the head of the baby into the chest of the mother, an effect reminiscent of Medardo Rosso's wax sculpture, in a plastic statement on a mother's protective role and the child's helpless dependence on her. Lehmbruck now felt isolated as an artist and despairing in the death and destruction of the war, in the cynical march of statesmen and kings over the bodies of their subjects—a theme explored in the *Macbeth* series of engravings —projected himself into the position of the child and was searching for the symbolic embrace of a new mother figure. This is suggested by his fascination with the actress Elisabeth Bergner and by the sculpture *Loving Heads*, which synthesizes the mother and child concept with the themes that had evolved in his prints, drawings and paintings. Gesture dominates here again, and in the overpowering concern with capturing the emotional content of the sculpture, formal structure is subordinate. The surfaces of the two faces are smooth, suggesting that had Lehmbruck truly finished this work he would have returned to the abstracting process that had culminated in the *Fallen Man* and the *Seated Youth*. The reduction of the two heads to ovals with only basic indications of lips and eyes suggest the path of intense formal reduction combined with passionately powerful expressive devices, which Brancusi had developed in the marble version of his *Prometheus*, and which Lehmbruck would have known from the 1912 Salon des Indépendants in which he also exhibited.

It is tempting to visualize the *Loving Heads* in marble rather than in bronze or plaster, since Lehmbruck demonstrated a new fascination with this material in the incomplete portrait of his wife and in a lost marble torso of the *Pensive Woman*. The stiff formality of the *Praying Girl* [55], also an unfinished sculpture, likewise may have its explanation in such an intended execution in marble. More than any other sculpture of his last year, this one suggests renewed plans for a monumental creation. Harshly tectonic and frontally conceived in a manner reminiscent of Egyptian sculpture, the figure is cut sharply from the surrounding space and her torso and arms appear as almost tubular substructures leading the viewer to a final confrontation with her head. She assumes a strange, overpowering presence unlike any of his earlier sculpture and points to new directions to explore, a path away from the despairing melancholy induced by the crises of war, toward a new faith and self-confidence. The path, however, was not to be taken.

"Style is fate: we cannot choose our own style," wrote Theodor Däubler. Lehmbruck's fate and his style appeared in the context of hopes for lasting peace and ultimate European coexistence, all of them destroyed by national searches for political greatness. As a result of World War I, not only Lehmbruck, but also his concept of Germany and Europe, of an artistic synthesis in an idealized and purified society, committed suicide. The destruction of his world and his resultant isolation led Lehmbruck to turn increasingly toward despair and to yearn for release through death. The poem "Who is still there?" provided his own epitaph; the goal for which his art consistently searched, the new international style of a new and unified art epoch, was not destined to be achieved.

footnotes

Works on Wilhelm Lehmbruck are cited in an abbreviated manner; for the full titles, see the bibliography.

1. Westheim, *Lehmbruck*. 1922, p. 9. Paul Westheim (1886–1963), German art historian and writer, defender and supporter of expressionism, wrote the first monograph on Lehmbruck (1919; revised ed., 1922), founder of the influential periodical *Das Kunstblatt* (published 1917–1933); emigrated to Paris in 1933, to Mexico in 1941.

2. *Caspar David Friedrich, Bekenntnisse*, K. K. Eberlein, ed. (Leipzig, 1924). The quotation is from the 1820s.

3. The usual date, 1905, assigned to this work is incorrect since the cast formerly in the collection of the Düsseldorf Academy is inscribed with the date 1902. On later casts, this date has been removed, probably by Lehmbruck himself. Why this was done is not clear.

4. Several other sculptors of Lehmbruck's generation likewise found it necessary to leave Germany for Paris between 1900 and 1914, in search of an artistic atmosphere conducive to the development of a new sculptural vocabulary. In addition to Lehmbruck, the most significant ones were Karl Albiker, Bernhard Hoetger, Georg Kolbe, Edwin Scharff, Hermann Haller and Ernesto di Fiori. In addition, the Parisian academies and salons attracted numerous German painters. Thus Lehmbruck followed his generation's general artistic move to Paris, a step taken by almost every major German artist since 1880 and thus again an action following an established pattern of artistic success.

5. Due to the narrowness of the central support which bears all the weight of the piece, most of the stone and plaster casts of the figure have broken at this point. The stone cast purchased at the Armory Show in 1913 had deteriorated by 1916; however, the bronze cast made from it (Museum of Modern Art, New York) loses all sense of the visual qualities of Lehmbruck's work primarily because of the loss of patinated surface. The same is true of other bronze casts with the exception of the cast in the Folkwang Museum, Essen; this suggests that this is the sole bronze cast of the *Standing Figure* made during Lehmbruck's lifetime.

6. Wilhelm Schäfer, "Wilhelm Lehmbruck," *Deutsche Monatshefte XV* (1915) pp. 292–300. Wilhelm Schäfer (1868–1952), writer and editor of the periodical *Die Rheinlande;* in Düsseldorf from 1900.

7. Julius Meier-Graefe (1867–1935), one of Germany's most significant and influential art critics and art historians. Co-founder in 1895 of the periodical *Pan* and author of *Die Entwicklungsgeschichte der Modernen Kunst* (Munich, 1904; Eng. trans.: *Modern Art*, New York, 1908) and author of significant monographs on Hans von Marées, Vincent van Gogh, Renoir, Cézanne, Manet, Delacroix, Menzel, Courbet and Degas.

8. Ernst Barlach in a conversation with Louis Tuaillon, February 1920, as cited by Friedrich Schult, *Ernst Barlach im Gespräch* (Munich, 1948), p. 120. The conversation was in specific reference to Lehmbruck's *Rising Youth*.

9. Theodor Däubler, *Der Neue Standpunkt* (Leipzig, 1919) pp. 187–8.

10. Paul Westheim, "Heimaturlaub zur Kunst: Zur Ausstellung der Freien Sezession in Berlin," *Frankfurter Zeitung*, No. 61, 2 March 1916.

Wilhelm Lehmbruck in his studio. Zurich, 1918

Catalog

catalog notes

With few exceptions, the exact dates when the sculptures of Wilhelm Lehmbruck were cast are not known. The documentation of casting dates is extremely difficult due to the unavailability or destruction of Lehmbruck family records and bronze foundry accounts. During World War II, the account and acquisition records of many German museums were destroyed, so that the purchase dates of Lehmbruck sculptures are not known; similarly, the antimodern art politics of the Third Reich deprived German museums (including the Duisburg City Museum) of their collection of Lehmbruck sculptures, and it has not always been possible to determine the fate of these earlier casts.

It has been possible, however, to determine a basic core of facts concerning the casts of Lehmbruck's sculpture. Most of the works created prior to 1918 were cast under the supervision of the artist or his wife in stone, plaster or terra-cotta; because of the expense, they were cast in bronze usually only after a commission had been received.

There is no indication that he attached specific aesthetic preferences to any material, but rather that casts in materials other than bronze were created for economic reasons. After the sculptor's suicide, his major works were cast in bronze (as well as a few examples in stone) by his widow. Judging from exhibition catalogs, most of these casts were made as early as 1919 or 1920, but some casts for the Lehmbruck family were produced later. Certain unauthorized, pirated casts, usually of poor quality, have also been made. All casts—stone and plaster as well as bronze—of Lehmbruck's 1918–19 works are posthumous.

As far as this information and the visual characteristics of casts from Lehmbruck's own lifetime make it possible to judge, the casts in this exhibition were all made during Lehmbruck's lifetime or the years immediately thereafter, with the known major exceptions of Catalog Numbers 6, 10, 22, 45 and 55.

R.H.

casts

The bronze foundries
whose marks are found on casts
of Lehmbruck's sculpture are:

Düsseldorfer Broncebildgiesserei,
G.m.b.H.
Düsseldorf-Obercassel.
*Founded in 1907 and operated until
1934. Apparently not used
by Lehmbruck after 1914.*
Erzgiesserei Bernhard Förster,
Düsseldorf-Obercassel.
*Founded in 1907 and operated until
1917. Apparently not used
by Lehmbruck after 1914.*
H. Gonot, Paris.
*Used solely during Lehmbruck's
time in Paris, 1910–1914.*
C. Valsuani, Paris.
*Used solely during Lehmbruck's
time in Paris, 1910–1914.*
Bildgiesserei Hermann Noack,
Berlin-Friedenau.
*Major German bronze foundry of
the 1910s and 1920s; still in
existence. Used by Lehmbruck and
his family beginning c. 1913.*
Erzgiesserei Ferdinand von Miller,
Munich.
*Sole known cast by this foundry is
the bronze of the Seated Youth,
purchased by the city of Duisburg
in 1929 but cast as early as 1919.*

*Entries in the catalog are arranged
chronologically. References to
exhibitions under each heading are
abbreviated and may be found in
detail in the exhibition listing
1906–1971. Insofar as was possible,
the material of the cast in previous
exhibitions is indicated. When material
is the same as the piece in
this exhibition, no medium is given.
Measurements are in millimeters
and inches and are given in this order:
height, width and depth and are taken
at the points of greatest extension.*

lenders to
the exhibition

The Family of the Artist, Stuttgart

Mrs. Lucie Figge, Düsseldorf

*Mr. and Mrs. J. H. Guttmann,
New York*

Kunsthalle, Karlsruhe

*Professor and Mrs. Andrew S. Keck,
Washington*

Wilhelm Lehmbruck Museum, Duisburg

Los Angeles County Museum of Art

Museum des 20. Jahrhunderts, Vienna

Nationalgalerie, Berlin

National Gallery of Art, Washington

Perry T. Rathbone, Boston

*Smith College Museum of Art,
Northampton*

*Steigenberger Hotel
Duisburger Hof, Duisburg*

Wallraf-Richartz Museum, Cologne

sculpture

1 SELF-PORTRAIT, 1898
Bronzed plaster
294 × 186 × 113 (11 9/16 × 7 5/16 × 4 7/16)
Signed on base, left: W. LEHMBRUCK
D'dorf. 1898
Collection: Wilhelm Lehmbruck Museum,
Duisburg
Provenance: Collection C. Nolden, Düsseldorf
Museumsverein Duisburg
Purchased 1930
Exhibitions:
Duisburg, 1969.

2 BATHING WOMAN, 1902
Bronze
660 × 381 × 238 (26 × 15 × 9 3/8)
Signed on base, top center: W. LEHMBRUCK

Collection: Mrs. Lucie Figge, Düsseldorf
Purchased 1970
Exhibitions:
*Cologne, 1906; Paris, Salon, 1907; Essen,
1907; Düsseldorf, 1908; Duisburg, 1929;
Bremen, 1956; Bielefeld, 1956; Amsterdam,
1956; Lübeck, 1956; Zurich, 1956;
Frankfurt, 1961; Antwerp, 1961; Munich,
1962; Vienna, 1963; Duisburg, 1964;
Duisburg, 1969.*

**3 STONE-ROLLER ("WORK"),
ca. 1903-05?**
Bronze on marble base
183 × 284 × 181 (7 3/16 × 11 3/16 × 7 1/8)
Signed on base: W. LEHMBRUCK
Foundry Mark: Bronceguss v.B. Förster,
Düsseldorf

Collection: Wilhelm Lehmbruck Museum,
Duisburg
Provenance: Collection C. Nolden, Düsseldorf
Museumsverein Duisburg
Purchased 1930
Exhibitions:
*Duisburg, 1929; Duisburg, 1964;
Duisburg, 1969 (Plaster).*

4 THE MINER, ca. 1903-1905?
Bronze relief
723 × 475 × 79 (28 1/2 × 18 11/16 × 3 1/8)
Signed lower right: W. LEHMBRUCK. DF.
Foundry Mark: Bronceguss B. Förster
Düsseldorf
Collection: Steigenberger Hotel
Duisburger Hof
Exhibitions:
*Essen, 1907; Duisburg, 1929;
Duisburg, 1964; Duisburg, 1969.*

**5 THE PATH TO BEAUTY:
PLAQUE HONORING
PROFESSOR SCHILL, 1905**
Bronze relief
324 × 241 × 12 (12 3/4 × 9 1/2 × 7/16)
Signed lower right: W. LEHMBRUCK
Collection: Wilhelm Lehmbruck Museum,
Duisburg
Provenance: Collection C. Nolden, Düsseldorf
Museumsverein Duisburg
Purchased 1930
Exhibitions:
*Düsseldorf, 1906; Paris, 1907; Düsseldorf,
1907; Essen, 1907; Berlin, 1908; Duisburg,
1929; Duisburg, 1964; Duisburg,
1969 (Plaster).*

6 **MOTHER AND CHILD, 1907**

Bronze

831 × 835 × 798 (32 3/4 × 32 7/8 × 31 3/8)

Collection: Wilhelm Lehmbruck Museum, Duisburg. Purchased 1964

Provenance: Family of the Artist

Exhibitions:

Paris, 1907 (Plaster); Düsseldorf, 1907 (Plaster); Munich, 1907 (Plaster); Cologne, 1908 (Plaster); Paris, 1910 (Plaster); Duisburg, 1929 (Plaster); Tübingen, 1948; Hannover, 1955; Frankfurt, 1961; Antwerp, 1961; Duisburg, 1964; Duisburg, 1969.

7 **MEDITATION: MOTHER AND CHILD, 1907**

Bronze relief

650 × 545 × 250 (25 5/8 × 21 1/2 × 9 13/16)

Signed on the base, front: W. LEHMBRUCK. DF. 07.

Foundry Mark: DUSSELDF. BRONCEBILD-GIESSEREI G.M.B.H.

Collection: Wilhelm Lehmbruck Museum, Duisburg

Provenance: Collection C. Nolden, Düsseldorf
Museumsverein Duisburg
Purchased 1929

Exhibitions:

Düsseldorf, 1907; Munich, 1907 (Plaster); Essen, 1907; Berlin, 1909; Düsseldorf, Exhibition of Christian Art, 1909; Duisburg, 1929; London, 1957; Leeds, 1957; Berlin, 1957; Duisburg, 1964; Duisburg, 1969.

8 **FEMALE FIGURE II, Competition Entry for a Façade Figure for the Tietz Department Store, Düsseldorf, 1908**

Bronze

375 × 95 × 75 (14 7/8 × 3 3/4 × 2 15/16)

Signed on base, left: W. LEHMBRUCK

Collection: Wilhelm Lehmbruck Museum, Duisburg

Provenance: Museumsverein Duisburg
Purchased 1930

Exhibitions:

Duisburg, 1964; Duisburg, 1969.

9 **GRIEVING WOMAN, 1909**

Bronze relief

785 × 454 × 45 (30 7/8 × 17 7/8 × 1 3/4)

Signed lower right: W. LEHMBRUCK 1909

Foundry Marks: DUSSELDORFER BRONCEGIESSEREI G.M.B.H.

Collection: Wilhelm Lehmbruck Museum, Duisburg. Purchased 1955

Provenance: Collection C. Nolden, Düsseldorf
Galerie Abels, Cologne

Exhibitions:

Düsseldorf, Exhibition of Christian Art, 1909; Paris, Salon d'Automne, 1909; Duisburg, 1929; Berlin, 1957; Duisburg, 1964; Duisburg, 1969.

10 **STANDING FEMALE FIGURE, 1910**

Bronze

1965 × 540 × 399 (75 1/4 × 21 1/4 × 15 3/4)

Signed on base, left: W. LEHMBRUCK. 1910 PARIS

Collection: National Gallery of Art, Washington, Ailsa Mellon Bruce Fund
Purchased 1965

Provenance: Family of the Artist

Exhibitions:
*Paris, 1910 (Plaster); Paris, 1911 (Plaster);
Paris, 1911 (Plaster); Munich, 1911
(Plaster); Düsseldorf, 1911 (Plaster);
Cologne, 1912 (Stone); New York, 1913
(Stone); Baden-Baden, 1913 (Stone); Chicago,
1913 (Stone); Boston, 1913 (Stone);
Mannheim, 1913 (Stone); Berlin, 1914 (Stone);
Paris, 1914 (Plaster); Mannheim, 1916
(Stone); Basel, 1917 (Marble); Berlin, 1920;
Munich, 1921; Duisburg, 1925 (Marble);
Cologne, 1925 (Marble); Duisburg, 1929
(Marble); New York, 1930; New York, 1939;
Tübingen, 1948; Bern, 1948 (Plaster);
Mannheim, 1949 (Stone); Düsseldorf, 1949
(Stone); Hamburg, 1949 (Stone); Stuttgart,
1949 (Stone); New York, 1951; Hannover,
1955; Duisburg, 1955 (Marble); Bremen,
1956; Bielefeld, 1956; Amsterdam, 1956;
Lübeck, 1956; Zurich, 1956; London, 1957;
Leeds, 1957; Berlin, 1957; St. Louis, 1957;
Antwerp, 1961; Frankfurt, 1961; Vienna,
1963; New York, 1963; Duisburg, 1964
(Plaster).*

11 FEMALE TORSO, 1910

Bronze
1180 high (46 ½)
Foundry Marks: H. NOACK BERLIN-FRIEDENAU
Collection: Wallraf-Richartz Museum,
          Cologne
Provenance: Family of the Artist
Exhibitions:
*Paris, Salon, 1911; Paris, 1911; Munich,
1911; Paris, 1911; Hagen, 1912; Cologne,
1912; Baden-Baden, 1913 (Stone);
Mannheim, 1916 (Stone); Munich, 1921;
Duisburg, 1925; Cologne, 1925; New York,
1939 (Stone); Tübingen, 1948 (Stone); Bern,
1948 (Stone); Mannheim, 1949 (Stone);
Düsseldorf, 1949 (Stone); Hamburg, 1949
(Stone); Stuttgart, 1949 (Stone); Amsterdam,
1956 (Stone); Munich, 1962 (Stone); Vienna,
1963 (Stone); Duisburg, 1964 (Stone);
Berlin (East), 1966 (Stone);
New York, 1969 (Stone).*

12 INCLINED HEAD OF A WOMAN, 1910

Cast stone
420 × 430 × 210 (16 ½ × 17 × 8 ¼)
Signed on the right shoulder: LEHMBRUCK
Collection: Family of the Artist
Exhibitions:
*Paris, 1911; Berlin, 1920 (Bronze); Munich,
1921; Duisburg, 1925 (Bronze); Cologne,
1925 (Bronze); Duisburg, 1929 (Bronze);
Tübingen, 1948 (Bronze); Mannheim, 1949
(Bronze); Düsseldorf, 1949 (Bronze);
Hamburg, 1949 (Bronze); Stuttgart, 1949
(Bronze); Washington, 1952; Hannover 1955;
Bremen 1956 (Bronze); Bielefeld, 1956
(Bronze); Amsterdam, 1956 (Bronze);
Lübeck, 1956 (Bronze); Zurich, 1956 (Bronze);
Frankfurt, 1961 (Bronze); Antwerp, 1961
(Bronze); New York, 1961; Munich, 1962
(Bronze); Vienna, 1963 (Bronze);
Duisburg, 1964 (Bronze).*

13 BUST OF FRAU LEHMBRUCK, 1910

Bronze
797 × 544 × 289 (31⅜ × 21⅜ × 11⅜)
Signed on the back, left: LEHMBRUCK
    (Under left arm, remainder of an erased
    signature: W . . . . . . L . H . . . . . .)
Collection: Wilhelm Lehmbruck Museum,
          Duisburg. Purchased 1964
Provenance: Family of the Artist
Exhibitions:
*Paris, 1911; Hagen, 1912; Cologne, 1912;
Paris, 1914 (Stone); Berlin, 1920 (Bronze and
Stone); Munich, 1921 (Bronze and Stone);
Duisburg, 1925; Cologne, 1925; Duisburg,
1929; New York, 1939 (Bronze and Stone);
Tübingen, 1948; Bern, 1948; Mannheim,
1949; Düsseldorf, 1949; Hamburg, 1949;
Stuttgart, 1949; Hannover, 1955; Bremen,
1956; Bielefeld, 1956; Amsterdam, 1956;
Lübeck, 1956; Zurich, 1956; London, 1956;
Leeds, 1956; Berlin, 1956; Frankfurt, 1961;
Antwerp, 1961; Munich, 1962; Vienna, 1963;
New York, 1963; Duisburg, 1964 (Bronze
and Stone).*

14 PORTRAIT HEAD OF
FRAU LEHMBRUCK, 1910

Gray stone
510 × 641 × 375 (20 ⅛ × 25 ¼ × 14 ¾)
Collection: Wilhelm Lehmbruck Museum,
   Duisburg. Purchased 1930
Provenance: Collection Leo Habig,
   Herdecke/Ruhr
Exhibitions:
*Paris, 1914; Berlin, 1920 (Marble, stone, and
bronze); Munich, 1921 (Marble and stone);
Duisburg, 1925 (Bronze); Berlin, 1929
(Bronze); Duisburg, 1929 (Bronze);
Tübingen, 1948 (Bronze); Mannheim, 1949
(Bronze); Düsseldorf, 1949 (Bronze);
Hamburg, 1949 (Bronze); Stuttgart, 1949
(Bronze); Hannover, 1955 (Bronze); Bremen,
1956 (Bronze); Bielefeld, 1956 (Bronze);
Amsterdam, 1956 (Bronze); Lübeck, 1956
(Bronze); Zurich, 1956 (Bronze); London,
1957 (Bronze); Leeds, 1957 (Bronze);
Berlin, 1957 (Bronze); Frankfurt, 1961
(Bronze); Antwerp, 1961 (Bronze); Munich,
1962 (Bronze); Vienna, 1963 (Bronze);
New York, 1963 (Stone?); Duisburg, 1964.*

15 GIRL RESTING, 1910

Bronze
642 × 185 × 185 (25 ¼ × 7 ¼ × 7 ¼)
Signed on base, back: W. LEHMBROCK (sic)
     PARIS
Foundry Mark: H. GONOT FONDEUR PARIS
Collection: Wilhelm Lehmbruck Museum,
   Duisburg
Provenance: Collection C. Nolden, Düsseldorf
   Museumsverein Duisburg
   Purchased 1930
Exhibitions:
*Munich, 1921; Duisburg, 1929; New York,
1939; Tübingen, 1948; Mannheim, 1949;
Düsseldorf, 1949; Hamburg, 1949; Stuttgart,
1949; Hannover, 1955; Bremen, 1956;*

*Bielefeld, 1956; Amsterdam, 1956; Lübeck,
1956; Zurich, 1956; London, 1956; Leeds,
1956; Berlin, 1957; Recklinghausen,
1958; Frankfurt, 1961; Antwerp, 1961;
Munich, 1962; Vienna, 1963; New York,
1963; Duisburg, 1964.*

16 SEATED CHILD, 1910

Bronze
646 × 440 × 337 (25 ⅜ × 17 ⁵⁄₁₆ × 13 ¼)
Signed on base, back: LEHMBRUCK
Collection: Family of the Artist
Exhibitions:
*Paris, 1914 (Plaster); Mannheim, 1916;
Munich, 1921; Duisburg, 1929; Tübingen,
1948; Mannheim, 1949; Düsseldorf, 1949;
Hamburg, 1949; Stuttgart, 1949; Hannover,
1955; Bremen, 1956; Bielefeld, 1956;
Amsterdam, 1956; Lübeck, 1956; Zurich,
1956; London, 1957; Leeds, 1957; Berlin,
1957; Frankfurt, 1961; Antwerp, 1961;
Munich, 1962; Vienna, 1963; Duisburg, 1964.*

17 SMALL FEMALE TORSO, 1910/11

Gray stone
700 × 230 × 241 (27 ½ × 9 ¹⁄₁₆ × 9 ½)
Signed on base, back: LEHMBRUCK
Collection: Family of the Artist
Exhibitions:
*Paris, Salon d'Automne, 1911; Hagen, 1912;
Paris, 1914; Berlin, 1920 (Stone and bronze);
Munich, 1921; Duisburg, 1925 (Bronze);
Cologne, 1925 (Bronze); Duisburg, 1929
(Bronze); New York, 1939; Tübingen, 1948
(Bronze); Cologne, 1948; Bern, 1948 (Bronze);
Mannheim, 1949 (Bronze); Düsseldorf, 1949
(Bronze); Hamburg, 1949 (Bronze); Stuttgart,
1949 (Bronze); New York, 1951 (Bronze);
Hannover, 1955; Bremen, 1956 (Bronze);*

*Bielefeld, 1956 (Bronze); Amsterdam, 1956
(Bronze); Lübeck, 1956 (Bronze); Zurich,
1956 (Bronze); London, 1957 (Bronze); Leeds,
1957 (Bronze); Berlin, 1957 (Bronze);
Frankfurt, 1961 (Bronze); Antwerp, 1961
(Bronze); Munich, 1962 (Bronze); Vienna,
1963 (Bronze); New York, 1963; Duisburg,
1964 (Bronze); Düsseldorf, 1969.*

*(Bronze and stone); Duisburg, 1925; Cologne,
1925; Duisburg, 1929; New York, 1939
(Stone); Tübingen, 1948; Bern, 1948;
Mannheim, 1949; Düsseldorf, 1949;
Hamburg, 1949; Stuttgart, 1949; New York,
1951 (Stone); Hannover, 1955; Bremen, 1956;
Bielefeld, 1956; Amsterdam, 1956; Lübeck,
1956; Zurich, 1956; New York, Knoedler,
1957; Cambridge, 1957; St. Louis, 1957
(Stone); Recklinghausen, 1958; Frankfurt,
1961; Antwerp, 1961; Munich, 1962; Vienna,
1963; New York, 1963 (Stone); Duisburg,
1964 (Plaster and bronze); Berlin (East), 1966.*

18   **TEMPTATION, 1911**
Bronze relief
515 × 310 × 35 (20 ¼ × 12 ³/₁₆ × 1 ⅜)
Signed lower right: LEHMBRUCK PARIS
Collection: Wilhelm Lehmbruck Museum,
       Duisburg
Provenance: Collection C. Nolden, Düsseldorf
       Museumsverein Duisburg
       Purchased 1930
Exhibitions:
*Paris, 1914 (Terra-cotta); Düsseldorf, 1919
(Terra-cotta); Duisburg, 1929; Mannheim,
1949; Düsseldorf, 1949; Hamburg, 1949;
Stuttgart, 1949; Hannover, 1955; Bremen,
1956; Bielefeld, 1956; Amsterdam, 1956;
Lübeck, 1956; Zurich, 1956; London, 1957;
Leeds, 1957; Berlin, 1957; Frankfurt, 1961;
Antwerp, 1961; Munich, 1962;
Vienna, 1963; Duisburg, 1964.*

20   **STATUETTE OF
A PENSIVE WOMAN, 1911**
Stone cast
550 × 160 × 150 (20 ⅝ × 6 ⅞ × 6 ¼)
Collection: Perry T. Rathbone, Boston

21   **STATUETTE OF
A PENSIVE WOMAN, 1911**
Plaster (not illustrated)
550 × 160 × 150 (20 ⅝ × 6 ⅞ × 6 ¼)
Collection: Wilhelm Lehmbruck Museum,
       Duisburg
(Exhibited only in Washington)

19   **STATUETTE OF
A PENSIVE WOMAN, 1911**
Bronze
525 × 175 × 159 (20 ⅝ × 6 ⅞ × 6 ¼)
Signed on base, back: LEHMBRUCK
Signed on base, front: LEHMBROCK (sic)
Foundry Mark: GUSS NOACK BERLIN
Collection: Family of the Artist
Exhibitions:
*Düsseldorf, 1911 (Plaster); Hagen, 1912;
Paris, 1914; Berlin, 1920; Munich, 1921*

22   **KNEELING WOMAN, 1911**
Bronze
1780 × 141 × 710 (70 × 55 ½ × 28)
Signed on base, left: LEHMBRUCK
Collection: Family of the Artist, on loan to the
       Museum des 20. Jahrhunderts,
       Vienna

Exhibitions:
*Paris, Salon d'Automne 1911 (Plaster);
Berlin, 1912 (Plaster); Cologne, 1912
(Stone); New York, 1913 (Stone); Chicago,
1913 (Stone); Boston, 1913 (Stone); Paris,
1914 (Plaster); Mannheim, 1916 (Stone);
Zurich, 1917 (Stone); Basel, 1917
(Stone); Berlin, 1920 (Stone and bronze);
Munich, 1921; Duisburg, 1925; Cologne,
1925; Duisburg, 1929; New York, 1939
(Stone); Philadelphia, 1941 (Stone);
Richmond, 1941 (Stone); Tübingen, 1948;
Bern, 1948 (Plaster); Mannheim, 1949;
Düsseldorf, 1949; Hamburg, 1949; Stuttgart,
1949; London, 1951; Hannover, 1955;
Duisburg, 1955; Bremen, 1956; Bielefeld,
1956; Amsterdam, 1956; Lübeck, 1956;
Zurich, 1956; London, 1957; Leeds, 1957;
Berlin, 1957; New York, 1958 (Stone);
Frankfurt, 1961; Antwerp, 1961; Munich,
1962; Vienna, 1963; Cassel, 1964;
Duisburg, 1964 (Plaster and bronze).*

23 HEAD OF KNEELING
WOMAN, 1911
Bronze
428 × 421 × 191 (16 ⅞ × 16 ⁹⁄₁₆ × 7 ½)
Signed on back, right: W. LEHMBRUCK
Foundry Mark: CIRE VALSUANI PERDUE
Collection: Wilhelm Lehmbruck Museum,
      Duisburg. Purchased 1964
Provenance: Family of the Artist
Exhibitions:
*Paris, Salon d'Automne 1911;
Cologne, 1912; Cologne, 1913; Baden-
Baden, 1913; Mannheim, 1913; Mannheim,
1914 (Terra-cotta); Munich, 1914
(Terra-cotta); Paris, 1914 (Stone);
Mannheim, 1916; Basel, 1917; Zurich, 1919;
Bern, 1919; Berlin, 1920; Darmstadt, 1920;
Duisburg, 1925; Cologne, 1925; Duisburg,
1929; New York, 1930 (Terra-cotta);
New York, 1939 (Stone); Tübingen, 1948;*

*Mannheim, 1949; Düsseldorf, 1949;
Hamburg, 1949; Stuttgart, 1949; New York,
1951 (Stone); Hannover, 1955; Bremen, 1956;
Bielefeld, 1956; Amsterdam, 1956 (Bronze
and stone); Lübeck, 1956; Zurich, 1956;
London, 1957; Leeds, 1957; Berlin, 1957;
Frankfurt, 1961; Antwerp, 1961; Munich,
1962; Vienna, 1963; New York, 1963 (Stone);
Duisburg, 1964 (Terra-cotta and bronze).*

24 HEAD OF AN OLD WOMAN, 1913
Plaster tinted red
520 × 135 × 190 (20 ⅝ × 5 ⅜ × 7 ¾)
Signed on base, left: W. LEHMBRUCK
Collection: Wilhelm Lehmbruck Museum,
      Duisburg
Provenance: Museumsverein Duisburg
      Purchased 1926
Exhibitions:
*Duisburg, 1929; Hannover, 1955; Duisburg,
1955; Bremen, 1956 (Stone); Bielefeld, 1956
(Stone); Amsterdam, 1956 (Stone); Lübeck,
1956 (Stone); Zurich, 1956 (Stone); London,
1957; Leeds, 1957; Berlin, 1957; Frankfurt,
1961; Antwerp, 1961; Munich, 1962;
Vienna, 1963; Duisburg, 1964.*

25 BOWING FEMALE TORSO, 1913
Bronze
820 high (32 ¼)
Collection: Kunsthalle, Karlsruhe
Exhibitions:
*Mannheim, 1913 (Stone); Mannheim, 1914;
Mannheim, 1916; Berlin, 1920; Munich,
1921; Duisburg, 1925; Cologne, 1925;
Duisburg, 1929; New York, 1939 (Stone);
Tübingen, 1948; Bern, 1948; Mannheim,
1949; Düsseldorf, 1949; Hamburg, 1949;*

Stuttgart, 1949; Hannover, 1955; Duisburg,
1955; Bremen, 1955; Bielefeld, 1956;
Amsterdam, 1956; Lübeck, 1956; Zurich,
1956; London, 1957; Leeds, 1957; Berlin,
1957; St. Louis, 1957 (Terra-cotta);
Washington, 1958; Frankfurt, 1961;
Antwerp, 1961; Munich, 1962; Vienna, 1963;
New York, 1963 (Stone); New York, 1963
(Stone); Duisburg, 1964.

26 **BOWING FEMALE TORSO, 1913**

Bronze

820 high (32 ¼)

Collection: Andrew S. Keck, Washington
Purchased 1945

Provenance: E. Weyhe

27 **RISING YOUTH, 1913**

Bronze

2280 × 760 × 620 (89 × 37 ¾ × 22¹¹/₁₆)

Signed on base, top left: W. LEHMBRUCK

Foundry Mark: H. NOACK BERLIN-FRIEDENAU

Collection: Family of the Artist

Exhibitions:

Berlin, 1916 (Stone); Mannheim, 1916 (Stone);
Darmstadt, 1918 (Stone); Berlin, 1920;
Munich, 1921; Duisburg, 1925; Cologne,
1925; Duisburg, 1929; New York, 1939
(Stone); Tübingen, 1948; Bern, 1948;
Mannheim, 1949; Düsseldorf, 1949;
Hamburg, 1949; Stuttgart, 1949; Hannover,
1955; Duisburg, 1955; Bremen, 1956;
Bielefeld, 1956; Amsterdam, 1956; Zurich,
1956; London, 1957; Leeds, 1957; Berlin,
1957; New York, 1957 (Stone); Frankfurt,
1961; Antwerp, 1961; Munich, 1962;
Vienna, 1963; Duisburg, 1964.

28 **HEAD OF THE
RISING YOUTH, 1913**

Terra-cotta

497 × 470 × 317 (19 ⅝ × 18 ½ × 12 ½)

Collection: Family of the Artist

Exhibitions:

Berlin, 1920 (Bronze); Munich, 1921;
Duisburg, 1925 (Bronze); Cologne, 1925
(Bronze); Duisburg, 1929 (Bronze);
New York, 1930 (Stone); New York, 1939
(Stone); Tübingen, 1948 (Bronze); Mannheim,
1949 (Bronze); Düsseldorf, 1949 (Bronze);
Hamburg, 1949 (Bronze); Stuttgart, 1949
(Bronze); New York, 1951 (Stone); Hannover,
1955 (Bronze); Duisburg, 1955 (Bronze);
Bremen, 1956 (Bronze); Bielefeld, 1956
(Bronze); Amsterdam, 1956 (Bronze);
Lübeck, 1956 (Bronze); Zurich, 1956 (Bronze);
London, 1957 (Bronze); Leeds, 1957
(Bronze); Berlin, 1957 (Bronze); Frankfurt,
1961 (Bronze); Antwerp, 1961 (Bronze);
Munich, 1962 (Bronze); Vienna, 1963
(Bronze); New York, 1963 (Stone); Duisburg,
1964 (Bronze and terra-cotta).

29 **TORSO OF A GIRL LOOKING
OVER HER SHOULDER, 1913/14**

Red stone

980 × 340 × 362 (38 ⅝ × 13 ⅜ × 14 ¼)

Signed on back: W. LEHMBRUCK

Collection: Family of the Artist

Exhibitions:

Paris, 1914; Mannheim, 1916; Berlin,
1919; Berlin, 1920 (Bronze and stone);
Darmstadt, 1920; Munich, 1921; Duisburg,
1925 (Bronze); Cologne, 1925 (Bronze);
Duisburg, 1929 (Bronze); Tübingen, 1948
(Bronze); Bern, 1948 (Bronze); Mannheim,
1949 (Bronze); Düsseldorf, 1949 (Bronze);
Hamburg, 1949 (Bronze); Stuttgart, 1949
(Bronze); Amsterdam, 1956 (Bronze); Lübeck,
1956 (Bronze); Zurich, 1956 (Bronze);
London, 1957; Leeds, 1957; Berlin, 1957;
Frankfurt, 1961 (Bronze); Antwerp, 1961
(Bronze); New York, 1961; Munich, 1962
(Bronze); Vienna, 1963 (Bronze); Duisburg,
1964; Cassel, 1964 (Bronze).

30 HEAD OF A GIRL LOOKING
OVER HER SHOULDER, 1913/14

Bronze

430 × 290 × 190 (17 × 11 3/8 × 7 1/2)

Signed on back: LEHMBRUCK (reversed)

Foundry Mark: H. NOACK BERLIN-FRIEDENAU

Collection: Family of the Artist

Exhibitions:

Munich, 1916 (Terra-cotta); Basel, 1917;
Berlin, 1921; Munich, 1921; Duisburg, 1925;
Cologne, 1925; Duisburg, 1929; Tübingen,
1948; Mannheim, 1949; Düsseldorf, 1949;
Hamburg, 1949; Stuttgart, 1949; Hannover,
1955; Duisburg, 1955; Bremen, 1956;
Bielefeld, 1956; Amsterdam, 1956; Lübeck,
1956; Zurich, 1956; London, 1957; Leeds,
1957; Berlin, 1957; Frankfurt, 1961;
Antwerp, 1961; Munich, 1962; Vienna, 1963;
Duisburg, 1964.

31 PENSIVE WOMAN, 1913/14

Bronze

2080 × 420 × 430 (81 × 16 1/2 × 17)

Signed on base, left: W. LEHMBRUCK

Foundry Mark: H. NOACK BERLIN-FRIEDENAU

Collection: Family of the Artist, on loan to
the Nationalgalerie, Berlin

Exhibitions:

Paris, 1914 (Plaster); Mannheim, 1916
(Stone); Zurich, 1919 (Stone and Bronze);
Bern, 1919; Berlin, 1920; Darmstadt, 1920;
Munich, 1921; Duisburg, 1925; Cologne,
1925; Duisburg, 1929; Tübingen, 1948; Bern,
1948; Mannheim, 1949; Düsseldorf, 1949;
Hamburg, 1949; Stuttgart, 1949; Hannover,
1955; Duisburg, 1955; Bremen, 1956;
Bielefeld, 1956; Amsterdam, 1956; Lübeck,
1956; Zurich, 1956; London, 1957; Leeds,
1957; Berlin, 1957; Frankfurt, 1961;
Antwerp, 1961; Munich, 1962; Vienna, 1963;
Duisburg, 1964; Cassel, 1964 (Plaster).

32 TORSO OF THE
PENSIVE WOMAN, 1913/14

Bronze

1360 high (53 1/2)

Collection: Family of the Artist, on loan to
the Los Angeles County Museum

Exhibitions:

Mannheim, 1916 (Stone); Berlin, 1920 (Stone);
Munich, 1921; Duisburg, 1925 (Stone);
Cologne, 1925 (Stone); Duisburg, 1929 (Stone);
New York, 1930 (Stone); New York, 1939
(Stone); New York, 1941 (Stone).

33 TORSO OF THE
PENSIVE WOMAN, 1913/14

Stone cast

1015 high (40)

Collection: Smith College Museum of Art,
Northampton. Purchased 1922

Provenance: Collection Stephen Bourgeois

34 HEAD OF A WOMAN WITH
A SLENDER NECK, 1913/14

Bronze

400 × 260 × 170 (15 9/16 × 10 1/2 × 6 1/2)

Signed on neck, back: W. LEHMBRUCK

Foundry Stamp: CIRE

C. VALSUANI

PERDUE

Collection: Wilhelm Lehmbruck Museum,
Duisburg. Purchased 1954

Provenance: Frankfurter Kunstkabinett,
Frankfurt

Exhibitions:

Paris, 1914; Mannheim, 1916; Zurich, 1917;
(Stone); Basel, 1917; Zurich, 1919; Bern,
1919; Berlin, 1920; Darmstadt, 1920;
Munich, 1921; Duisburg, 1925; Cologne,
1925; Duisburg, 1929; Tübingen, 1948;
Mannheim, 1949; Düsseldorf, 1949;

*Hamburg, 1949; Stuttgart, 1949; Hannover,
1955; Amsterdam, 1956 (Stone); Lübeck,
1956 (Stone); Zurich, 1956 (Stone); London,
1957 (Stone); Leeds, 1957 (Stone); Berlin,
1957; Recklinghausen, 1958; Frankfurt,
1961; Antwerp, 1961; Duisburg, 1964.*

35   **SEATED GIRL, 1913/14**
Bronze
290 × 470 × 210 (11 ½ × 18 ½ × 8 ¼)
Signed on base, front: W. LEHMBRUCK
Signed on base, back: W. Lehmbruck
Collection: Family of the Artist
Exhibitions:
*Paris, 1914; Berlin, 1916 (Stone); Mannheim,
1916; Berlin, 1920; Munich, 1921; Duisburg,
1925; Cologne, 1925; Duisburg, 1929;
New York, 1939; New York, 1939 (Stone);
Tübingen, 1948; Mannheim, 1949;
Düsseldorf, 1949; Hamburg, 1949; Stuttgart,
1949; New York, 1951 (Stone); Hannover,
1955 (Stone); Duisburg, 1955 (Stone); Bremen,
1956 (Stone); Bielefeld, 1956 (Stone);
Amsterdam, 1956 (Plaster); Lübeck, 1956
(Plaster); Zurich, 1956 (Plaster); London,
1957; Leeds, 1957; Berlin, 1957; Frankfurt,
1961 (Stone); Antwerp, 1961 (Stone); Munich,
1962; Vienna, 1963; New York, 1963 (Stone);
Duisburg, 1964; New York, 1969 (Stone).*

36   **BATHING GIRL, 1914**
Bronze
920 × 390 × 350 (36 ¼ × 15 ⅜ × 13 ¾)
Signed on base, right: W. LEHMBRUCK
Foundry Mark: H. NOACK
                BRONCEGIESSEREI
Collection: Family of the Artist

Exhibitions:
*Paris, 1914 (Stone); Mannheim, 1916 (Stone);
Zurich, 1917 (Stone); Basel, 1917 (Stone);
Berlin, 1920; Munich, 1921; Duisburg, 1925;
Cologne, 1925; Duisburg, 1929; New York,
1930 (Stone); Tübingen, 1948; Bern, 1948;
Mannheim, 1949; Düsseldorf, 1949;
Hamburg, 1949; Stuttgart, 1949; New York,
1951; Hannover, 1955; Duisburg, 1955;
Bremen, 1956; Bielefeld, 1956; Amsterdam,
1956; Lübeck, 1956; Zurich, 1956; London,
1957; Leeds, 1957; Berlin, 1957; Frankfurt,
1961; Antwerp, 1961; Munich, 1962; Vienna,
1963; New York, 1963; Duisburg, 1964
(Stone); Berlin (East), 1966 (Stone).*

37   **THREE WOMEN, RELIEF, 1914**
Bronze
980 × 680 (38 ⅝ × 26 ¾)
Foundry Mark: H. NOACK
                BERLIN-FRIEDENAU
Collection: Family of the Artist
Exhibitions:
*Paris, 1914 (Terra-cotta); Berlin, 1920;
Munich, 1921; Duisburg, 1925; Cologne,
1925; Duisburg, 1929; Tübingen, 1948; Bern,
1948; Mannheim, 1949; Düsseldorf, 1949;
Hamburg, 1949; Stuttgart, 1949; Hannover,
1955; Duisburg, 1955; Bremen, 1956;
Bielefeld, 1956; London, 1957; Leeds, 1957;
Berlin, 1957; Frankfurt, 1961; Antwerp,
1961; Munich, 1962; Vienna, 1963;
Duisburg, 1964 (Stone).*

38   **GIRL LOOKING OVER
HER SHOULDER, 1914/15**
Bronze
915 × 245 × 290 (36 1/16 × 9 ⅝ × 11 ⅜)
Signed on base, left: W. LEHMBRUCK
Foundry Mark: H. NOACK
                BERLIN-FRIEDENAU

Collection: Wilhelm Lehmbruck Museum,
Duisburg
Provenance: Museumsverein Duisburg.
Purchased 1928
Exhibitions:
*Mannheim, 1916 (Stone); Basel, 1917 (Stone);
Berlin, 1918 (Stone); Zurich, 1919; Berlin,
1919 (Terra-cotta?); Düsseldorf, 1919 (Stone);
Düsseldorf, 1919 (Stone); Bern, 1919; Berlin,
1920; Darmstadt, 1920; Munich, 1921;
Cologne, 1925; Duisburg, 1925; Duisburg,
1929; New York, 1930 (Terra-cotta);
New York, 1939 (Stone); Tübingen, 1948
(Stone); Bern, 1948 (Stone); Mannheim, 1949
(Stone); Düsseldorf, 1949 (Stone); Hamburg,
1949 (Stone); Stuttgart, 1949 (Stone);
New York, 1951 (Stone); Hannover, 1955;
Duisburg, 1955; Bremen, 1956; Bielefeld,
1956; Amsterdam, 1956; Lübeck, 1956;
Zürich, 1956; London, 1957 (Stone); Leeds,
1957 (Stone); Berlin, 1957 (Stone); Frankfurt,
1961; Antwerp, 1961; Munich, 1962;
Vienna, 1963; New York, 1963 (Stone);
New York, 1963 (Stone); Duisburg, 1964.*

39 PORTRAIT OF HERR FALK, 1915/16

Stone
445 × 165 × 234 (17 ½ × 6 ½ × 9 ⅛)
Collection: Wilhelm Lehmbruck Museum,
Duisburg. Acquired 1964
Provenance: Collection Dr. Schäfer,
Schweinfurt

40 PORTRAIT OF HERR FALK, 1915

Bronze
550 high (21 ½)
Collection: Mr. and Mrs. J. H. Guttmann,
New York. Purchased 1970
Provenance: Tannenbaum Gallery, N.Y.
Collection Ernst Pinkus, N.Y.
Parke-Bernet

41 PORTRAIT BUST OF FRAU FALK, 1915/16

Red stone
620 × 320 × 290 (24 ⅜ × 12 ½ × 11 ⅜)
Collection: Family of the Artist
Exhibitions:
*Mannheim, 1916 (Marble); Basel, 1917;
Zurich, 1919; Berlin, 1920; Munich, 1921;
Duisburg, 1925; Cologne, 1925; Duisburg,
1929 (Marble); Tübingen, 1948; Mannheim,
1949; Düsseldorf, 1949; Hamburg, 1949;
Stuttgart, 1949; Hannover, 1955 (Marble);
Duisburg, 1955 (Marble); Bremen, 1956
(Marble); Bielefeld, 1956 (Marble);
Amsterdam, 1956 (Marble); Lübeck, 1956
(Marble); Zurich, 1956 (Marble); London,
1957 (Marble); Leeds, 1957 (Marble);
Berlin, 1957 (Marble); Frankfurt, 1961
(Marble); Antwerp, 1961 (Marble); Munich,
1962 (Marble); Vienna, 1963 (Marble);
Duisburg, 1964 (Marble).*

42 PORTRAIT BUST OF FRAU FALK, 1915/16

Bronze
650 high (25 ½)
Collection: Mr. and Mrs. J. H. Guttmann,
New York. Purchased 1970
Provenance: Tanenbaum Gallery, N.Y.
Collection Ernst Pinkus, N.Y.
Parke-Bernet

43 PORTRAIT BUST OF FRAU FALK, 1915/16

Marble
590 high (23 ¼)
Collection: Wilhelm Lehmbruck Museum,
Duisburg

44 PORTRAIT STATUETTE OF
FRAU FALK, 1915/16

Bronze
623 × 228 × 153 (24 ½ × 9 × 6)
Collection: Wilhelm Lehmbruck Museum,
Duisburg. Purchased 1964
Provenance: Family of the Artist
Exhibitions:
*Mannheim, 1916; Basel, 1917; Berlin, 1920;
Munich, 1921; Duisburg, 1925 (Stone);
Cologne, 1925 (Stone); Duisburg, 1929 (Stone);
Tübingen, 1948 (Terra-cotta); Bern, 1948
(Terra-cotta); Mannheim, 1949 (Terra-
cotta); Düsseldorf, 1949 (Terra-cotta);
Hamburg, 1949 (Terra-cotta); Stuttgart,
1949 (Terra-cotta); Hannover, 1955 (Terra-
cotta); Duisburg, 1955 (Terra-cotta); Bremen,
1956 (Terra-cotta); Bielefeld, 1956 (Terra-
cotta); Amsterdam, 1956 (Terra-cotta);
Lübeck, 1956 (Terra-cotta); Zurich, 1956
(Terra-cotta); London, 1957 (Terra-cotta);
Leeds, 1957 (Terra-cotta); Berlin, 1957
(Terra-cotta); Frankfurt, 1961; Antwerp,
1961; Munich, 1962; Vienna, 1963;
Duisburg, 1964 (Terra-cotta and bronze).*

45 FALLEN MAN, 1915/16

Bronze
780 × 2390 × 830 (30 ½ × 94 × 32 ¾)
Collection: Family of the Artist, on loan to
the National Gallery, Berlin
Exhibitions:
*Berlin, 1916 (Plaster); Berlin, 1920 (Stone);
Munich, 1921; Duisburg, 1925 (Stone);
Cologne, 1925 (Stone); Duisburg, 1929 (Stone);
Tübingen, 1948 (Plaster); Bern, 1948
(Plaster); Mannheim, 1949 (Plaster);
Düsseldorf, 1949 (Plaster); Hamburg, 1949
(Plaster); Stuttgart, 1949 (Plaster); Hannover
1955 (Stone); Duisburg, 1955 (Stone);
Bremen, 1956 (Stone); Bielefeld, 1956 (Stone);
Amsterdam, 1956 (Stone); Lübeck, 1956
(Stone); Zurich, 1956 (Stone); London, 1957
(Stone); Leeds, 1957 (Stone); Berlin, 1957
(Stone); Frankfurt, 1961 (Stone); Antwerp,
1961 (Stone); Munich, 1962 (Stone); Vienna,
1963 (Stone); Duisburg, 1964 (Stone).*

46 PORTRAIT BUST OF
MISS K, 1916

Red stone
650 × 692 × 337 (25 ⅝ × 27 ¼ × 13 ¼)
Collection: Family of the Artist
Exhibitions:
*Duisburg, 1925; Cologne, 1925; Tübingen,
1948; Mannheim, 1949; Düsseldorf, 1949;
Hamburg, 1949; Stuttgart, 1949; Amsterdam,
1956; Lübeck, 1956; Zurich, 1956; London,
1957; Leeds, 1957; Berlin, 1957; Frankfurt,
1961; Antwerp, 1961; Munich, 1962;
Vienna, 1963; Duisburg, 1964.*

47 PORTRAIT OF FRITZ
VON UNRUH, 1917

Gray stone
540 × 244 × 216 (21 ¼ × 9 ⅝ × 8 ½)
Collection: Wilhelm Lehmbruck Museum,
Duisburg. Purchased 1964
Provenance: Family of the Artist
Exhibitions:
*Berlin, 1919; Bern, 1919; Berlin, 1920;
Munich, 1921; Duisburg, 1925; Cologne,
1925; Duisburg, 1929; Tübingen, 1948;
Mannheim, 1949; Düsseldorf, 1949;
Hamburg, 1949; Stuttgart, 1949; Amsterdam,
1956; Lübeck, 1956; Zurich, 1956; London,
1957; Leeds, 1957; Berlin, 1957; Frankfurt,
1961; Antwerp, 1961; Munich, 1962;
Vienna, 1963; Duisburg, 1964.*

48 SEATED YOUTH
(THE FRIEND), 1915-17

Bronze
1035 × 768 × 1148 (40 ¾ × 30 ¼ × 45 ¼)
Signed on base, left: LEHMBRUCK
Foundry Mark: GEGOSSEN ERZGIESSEREI
FERD. MILLER, MUNCHEN

Collection: Wilhelm Lehmbruck Museum,
Duisburg
Provenance: Museumsverein Duisburg
Purchased 1929
City Art Museum, Duisburg
Exhibitions:
*Basel, 1917; Berlin, 1918; Zurich, 1919;
Bern, 1919; Berlin, 1920; Munich, 1921;
Duisburg, 1925; Duisburg, 1929; New York,
Valentine Gallery, 1939 (Stone); Philadelphia,
1941 (Stone); Richmond, 1941 (Stone);
Tübingen, 1948; Hannover, 1955; Duisburg,
1955; Bremen, 1956; Bielefeld, 1956;
Amsterdam, 1956; Lübeck, 1956; Zurich,
1956; London, 1957; Leeds, 1957; Berlin,
1957; Frankfurt, 1961; Antwerp, 1961;
Munich, 1962; Vienna, 1963; Duisburg, 1964.*

49 PORTRAIT BUST OF MRS. B
(Version II), 1918

Red stone
375 high (14 ¾)
Collection: Family of the Artist
Exhibitions:
Duisburg, 1964.

50 HEAD OF FRAU LEHMBRUCK, 1918

Marble
534 × 255 × 267 (21 × 10 × 10 ½)
Collection: Wilhelm Lehmbruck Museum,
Duisburg. Purchased 1964
Provenance: Family of the Artist
Exhibitions:
*Tübingen, 1948; Bern, 1948; Mannheim,
1949; Düsseldorf, 1949; Hamburg, 1949;
Stuttgart, 1949; Hannover, 1955; Duisburg,
1955; Bremen, 1955; Bielefeld, 1956;
Amsterdam, 1956; Lübeck, 1956; Zurich,
1956; London, 1957; Leeds, 1957; Berlin,
1957; Frankfurt, 1961; Antwerp, 1961;
Munich, 1962; Vienna, 1963; Duisburg, 1964.*

51 FEMALE TORSO
(FRAGMENT), 1918

Bronze
780 × 430 × 190 (30 ¾ × 17 × 7 ½)
Collection: Family of the Artist
Exhibitions:
*Berlin, 1920 (Stone); Munich, 1921; Cologne,
1925 (Stone); Duisburg, 1925 (Stone);
Duisburg, 1929 (Stone); Tübingen, 1948
(Stone); Bern, 1948 (Stone); Mannheim, 1949
(Stone); Düsseldorf, 1949 (Stone); Hamburg,
1949 (Stone); Stuttgart, 1949 (Stone);
Hannover, 1955 (Stone); Duisburg, 1955
(Stone); Bremen, 1956 (Stone); Bielefeld, 1956
(Stone); Amsterdam, 1956 (Stone); Lübeck,
1956 (Stone); Zurich, 1956 (Stone); London,
1957 (Stone); Leeds, 1957 (Stone); Berlin,
1957 (Stone); Frankfurt, 1961; Munich, 1962;
Vienna, 1963; Duisburg, 1964 (Stone).*

52 MOTHER AND CHILD, 1918

Bronze
528 × 381 × 210 (20 ¾ × 15 × 8 ¼)
Foundry Mark: GUSS:
H. NOACK
FRIEDENAU-BERLIN
Collection: Wilhelm Lehmbruck Museum,
Duisburg
Provenance: Museumsverein Duisburg
Purchased 1928
Collection Frau Anita
Lehmbruck, Munich
Exhibitions:
*Bern, 1919; Berlin, 1920; Munich, 1921;
Duisburg, 1925; Cologne, 1925; Duisburg,
1929; New York, Harriman, 1939 (Stone);
Tübingen, 1948; Bern, 1948; Mannheim,
1949; Düsseldorf, 1949; Hamburg, 1949;
Stuttgart, 1949; Hannover, 1955 (Stone);
Duisburg, 1955; Bremen, 1956; Bielefeld,
1956; Amsterdam, 1956; Lübeck, 1956;
Zurich, 1956; London, 1957; Berlin, 1957;
Recklinghausen, 1958; Frankfurt, 1961;
Antwerp, 1961; Munich, 1962; Vienna, 1963;
New York, 1963 (Stone); New York, 1963
(Stone); Duisburg, 1964.*

53 HEAD OF A THINKER, (1918)

Bronze

645 × 572 × 298 (25 ⅜ × 22 ½ × 11 ¾)

Signed on left side: LEHMBRUCK

Foundry Mark: H. NOACK   BERLIN

Collection: Wilhelm Lehmbruck Museum,
Duisburg. Purchased 1964

Provenance: Family of the Artist

Exhibitions:

Berlin, 1919 (Stone); Berlin, 1920; Munich, 1921; Duisburg, 1925; Cologne, 1925; Duisburg, 1929; Tübingen, 1948 (Stone); Bern, 1948 (Stone); Mannheim, 1949 (Stone); Düsseldorf, 1949 (Stone); Hamburg, 1949 (Stone); Stuttgart, 1949 (Stone); New York, 1951 (Stone); Hannover, 1955 (Stone); Duisburg, 1955 (Stone); Bremen, 1956 (Stone); Bielefeld, 1956 (Stone); Amsterdam, 1956 (Stone); Lübeck, 1956 (Stone); Zurich, 1956 (Stone); London, 1957 (Stone); Leeds, 1957 (Stone); Berlin, 1957 (Stone); Frankfurt, 1961; Antwerp, 1961; Munich, 1962; Vienna, 1963; New York, 1963 (Stone); Duisburg, 1964.

54 LOVING HEADS, 1918

Bronze

830 × 500 × 310 (15 × 19 ¾ × 12 ¼)

Signed on base, left: LEHMBRUCK

Foundry Mark: H. NOACK   BERLIN

Collection: Family of the Artist

Exhibitions:

Berlin, 1920 (Stone); Munich, 1921; Duisburg, 1925 (Stone); Cologne, 1925 (Stone); Duisburg, 1929 (Stone); Tübingen, 1948 (Plaster); Bern, 1948 (Plaster); Mannheim, 1949 (Plaster); Düsseldorf, 1949 (Plaster); Hamburg, 1949 (Plaster); Stuttgart, 1949 (Plaster); Hannover, 1955 (Stone); Duisburg, 1955 (Stone); Bremen, 1956 (Stone); Bielefeld, 1956 (Stone); Amsterdam, 1956 (Stone); Lübeck, 1956 (Stone); Zurich, 1956 (Stone); London, 1957 (Stone); Leeds, 1957 (Stone); Berlin, 1957 (Stone); Frankfurt, 1961; Antwerp, 1961; Munich, 1962; Vienna, 1963; Duisburg, 1964 (Stone).

55 PRAYING GIRL, 1918

Bronze

840 × 550 × 400 (33 × 21 ⅝ × 15 ¾)

Collection: Family of the Artist

Exhibitions:

Bern, 1919; Berlin, 1920; Munich, 1921; Duisburg, 1925; Cologne, 1925; Duisburg, 1929 (Stone); Tübingen, 1948 (Stone); Bern, 1948 (Stone); Mannheim, 1949 (Stone); Düsseldorf, 1949 (Stone); Hamburg, 1949 (Stone); Stuttgart, 1949 (Stone); Hannover, 1955 (Stone); Duisburg, 1955 (Stone); Bremen, 1956 (Stone); Bielefeld, 1956 (Stone); Amsterdam, 1956 (Stone); Lübeck, 1956 (Stone); Zurich, 1956 (Stone); London, 1957 (Stone); Leeds, 1957 (Stone); Antwerp, 1961 (Stone); Frankfurt, 1961 (Stone); Munich, 1962 (Stone); Vienna, 1963 (Stone); Duisburg, 1964 (Stone).

paintings

56 MARTHA, 1912

Oil on canvas

960 × 610 (37 ¾ × 21)

Not signed or dated

Collection: Wilhelm Lehmbruck Museum,
Duisburg

Provenance: City Art Collection, Duisburg
Kunsthalle, Mannheim

Exhibitions:

Hannover, 1955; Duisburg, 1955; Bremen, 1956; Bielefeld, 1956; Amsterdam, 1956; Lübeck, 1956; Zurich, 1956; London, 1957; Leeds, 1957; Berlin, 1957; Recklinghausen, 1958; Antwerp, 1961; Frankfurt, 1961; Munich, 1962; Vienna, 1963; Duisburg, 1964.

57 PORTRAIT OF A WOMAN, 1912

Oil on canvas

990 × 770 (39 × 30 ⁵⁄₁₆)

Signed l.r.: W. Lehmbruck
Collection: Family of the Artist
Exhibitions:
Tübingen, 1948; Mannheim, 1949;
Düsseldorf, 1949; Hamburg, 1949; Stuttgart,
1949; Hannover, 1955; Duisburg, 1955;
Bremen, 1956; Bielefeld, 1956; Amsterdam,
1956; Lübeck, 1956; Zurich, 1956; London,
1957; Leeds, 1957; Berlin, 1957; Munich,
1962; Vienna, 1963; Duisburg, 1964.

58 SUSANNA, 1913

Oil on canvas
814 × 654 (32 × 25 ¾)
Signed l.r.: W. LEHMBRUCK
Collection: Wilhelm Lehmbruck Museum,
    Duisburg
Provenance: City Art Collection, Duisburg
    Collection Kirchhoff, Wiesbaden
Exhibitions:
Paris, 1913; Munich, 1915; Berlin, 1916;
Mannheim, 1916; Wiesbaden, 1917;
Hannover, 1955; Duisburg, 1955; Bremen,
1956; Bielefeld, 1956; Amsterdam, 1956;
Lübeck, 1956; Zurich, 1956; London, 1957;
Leeds, 1957; Berlin, 1957; Frankfurt, 1961;
Antwerp, 1961; Munich, 1962;
Vienna, 1963; Duisburg, 1964.

59 ABDUCTION, 1913

Oil on canvas
840 × 590 (33 ⅛ × 23 ¼)
Not signed or dated
Collection: Family of the Artist
Exhibitions:
Mannheim, 1916; Tübingen, 1948; Bern,
1948; Mannheim, 1949; Düsseldorf, 1949;

Hamburg, 1949; Stuttgart, 1949; Hannover,
1955; Duisburg, 1955; Bremen, 1956;
Bielefeld, 1956; Amsterdam, 1957; Lübeck,
1957; Zurich, 1957; Frankfurt, 1961;
Antwerp, 1961; Munich, 1962;
Vienna, 1963; Duisburg, 1964.

60 PIETÀ, 1915

Oil on canvas
730 × 540 (28 ¾ × 21 ¼)
Not signed or dated
Collection: Family of the Artist
Exhibitions:
Tübingen, 1948; Bern, 1948; Mannheim,
1949; Düsseldorf, 1949; Hamburg, 1949;
Stuttgart, 1949; Hannover, 1955; Duisburg,
1955; Bremen, 1956; Bielefeld, 1956;
Lübeck, 1956; Munich, 1962;
Vienna, 1963; Duisburg, 1964.

61 RECLINING FEMALE NUDE, 1916

Oil on canvas
720 × 530 (28 ⅜ × 20 ⅞)
Not signed or dated
Collection: Family of the Artist
Exhibitions:
Mannheim, 1949; Düsseldorf, 1949;
Hamburg, 1949; Stuttgart, 1949; Hannover,
1955; Duisburg, 1955; Bremen, 1956;
Bielefeld, 1956; Amsterdam, 1956; Lübeck,
1956; Zurich, 1956; Duisburg, 1964.

62 CROUCHING FEMALE NUDE, 1917

Oil on canvas
1200 × 960 (47 ¼ × 37 ¾)

Not signed or dated
Collection: Family of the Artist
Exhibitions:
*Tübingen, 1948; Bern, 1948; Hannover, 1955;
Duisburg, 1955; Bremen, 1956; Bielefeld,
1956; Amsterdam, 1956; Lübeck, 1956;
Zurich, 1956; London, 1957; Leeds, 1957;
Berlin, 1957; Frankfurt, 1961; Antwerp,
1961; Munich, 1962; Vienna, 1963;
Duisburg, 1964.*

drawings and pastels

63 **RECLINING BOY, 1897**
Red ochre on paper
260 × 605 (10 ⁵⁄₁₆ × 23¹³⁄₁₆)
Signed l.l.: W. Lehmbruck 97
Collection: Family of the Artist

64 **DRAWINGS FOR RICHARD
DEHMEL'S DIE MAGD, c. 1902**
Pencil, ink wash, pen and ink on cardboard
405 × 500 (16 × 19¹¹⁄₁₆)
Collection: Family of the Artist

65 **FIVE STUDIES FOR THE MINER,
c. 1903-05?**
Pencil on paper
420 × 290 (16 ½ × 11 ⅜)
Collection: Family of the Artist

66 **STUDY FOR MOTHER AND CHILD
AND PROJECT FOR A SCULPTURE:
CONSCIENCE: MOTHER WITH
DROWNED CHILD, c. 1905-06?**
330 × 210 (13 × 10 ⅜)
Pencil on paper
Collection: Family of the Artist

67 **SEATED CHILD, 1911**
Crayon on paper
220 × 171 (8 ⅝ × 6 ¾)
Collection: Family of the Artist, Inv. No. 287

68 **SKETCH FOR KNEELING WOMAN, 1911**
Pencil on cardboard
317 × 265 (12 ½ × 10 ⅜)
Collection: Family of the Artist, Inv. No. 300

69 **STANDING FEMALE NUDE
WITH DRAPERY, c. 1910-12?**
Ink wash on paper
312 × 233 (12 ¼ × 9 ⅛)
Collection: Family of the Artist, Inv. No. 616

70 **RECLINING NUDE, 1913**
Ink wash and pencil on cardboard
183 × 243 (7 ¼ × 9 ⅝)
Collection: Family of the Artist, Inv. No. 539

71 SEATED GIRL, 1913

Ink wash and pencil on cardboard

183 × 243 (7 ¼ × 9 ½)

Collection: Family of the Artist, Inv. No. 535

72 PENSIVE YOUTH, 1913

Sepia on paper

614 × 415 (24 3⁄16 × 16 ¼)

Signed l.r.: W. Lehmbruck

Collection: Family of the Artist, Inv. No. 527

73 MALE NUDE, c. 1913

Sepia on paper

610 × 410 (24 × 16 ⅛)

Signed l.r.: W. Lehmbruck

Collection: Wilhelm Lehmbruck Museum,
          Duisburg, Inv. No. 671/769

74 THREE FIGURES, 1913

Watercolor on paper

630 × 475 (24 ¾ × 18 ⅝)

Signed l.r.: W. Lehmbruck 1913

Collection: Wilhelm Lehmbruck Museum,
          Duisburg, Inv. No. 418/430

75 FALLEN FEMALE NUDE, c. 1913/14

Pastel on gray cardboard

710 × 990 (28 × 39)

Collection: Family of the Artist

76 FEMALE NUDE WITH
ARMS FOLDED, 1914

Crayon on paper

Signed l.l.: W. Lehmbruck

312 × 245 (12 ¼ × 9 ⅝)

Collection: Family of the Artist, Inv. No. 570

77 SKETCH FOR FALLEN MAN, 1915

Charcoal on paper

420 × 260 (16 ½ × 10 ¼)

Collection: Family of the Artist, Inv. No. 696

78 WOUNDED WARRIOR, c. 1915

Pencil on paper

270 × 220 (10 ⅝ × 8 ⅝)

Collection: Family of the Artist, Inv. No. 768

79 SKETCHES: THE YOUNG
REGIMENTS AND
THE LAST CRY, 1916

Crayon and pencil on paper

450 × 286 (17 ¾ × 11 ¼)

Collection: Family of the Artist, Inv. No. 782

80 SKETCH FOR FALLEN
MAN, c. 1916

Charcoal on paper

260 × 430 (10 ¼ × 17)

Signed l.r.: W. Lehmbruck

Collection: Wilhelm Lehmbruck Museum,
          Duisburg

81 EXHAUSTED WARRIOR, 1916
Pen and ink on paper
255 × 170 (10 × 6 ⅝)
Collection: Wilhelm Lehmbruck Museum,
    Duisburg, Inv. No. 579/663

82 AWAKENING WARRIOR
(RESURRECTION), 1916
Charcoal on paper
560 × 450 (22 × 17 ¾)
Collection: Family of the Artist, Inv. No. 732

83 FOUR CHARGING,
WOUNDED WARRIORS, 1916
Pencil and crayon on paper
281 × 226 (11 ⅛ × 8 ⅝)
Collection: Family of the Artist, Inv. No. 728

84 CONTEMPORARY PIETÀ, 1916
Crayon and pencil on paper
439 × 315 (17 ¼ × 12 ⅜)
Collection: Family of the Artist, Inv. No. 753

85 PORTRAIT OF THEODOR
DÄUBLER, 1916/17
Crayon on paper
330 × 210 (13 × 8 ¼)
Collection: Family of the Artist, Inv. No. 786

86 PIETÀ, 1917/18
Crayon on paper
278 × 214 (11 × 8 ⅜)
Collection: Family of the Artist, Inv. No. 817

87 PIETÀ, 1917/18
Crayon on paper
390 × 296 (15 ⅜ × 11 ⅝)
Collection: Family of the Artist, Inv. No. 807

88 PIETÀ, 1917/18
Crayon on paper
390 × 295 (15 ⅜ × 11 ⅝)
Collection: Family of the Artist, Inv. No. 822

89 HEAD OF A WOMAN,
PROFILE, 1918
Crayon on paper
390 × 295 (15 ⅜ × 11 ⅝)
Collection: Family of the Artist, Inv. No. 875

90 HEAD OF A WOMAN, 1918
Charcoal on paper
390 × 295 (15 ⅜ × 11 ⅝)
Collection: Family of the Artist, Inv. No. 879

91 SKETCH FOR LOVING HEADS
(LIPS CRADLED ON ARM), 1918
440 × 273 (17 ⅜ × 10 ¾)
Pencil on paper
Collection: Family of the Artist, Inv. No. 895

94 ABDUCTION II, PARTIAL
VIEW OF WOMAN, 1911
P 10 (not illustrated)
293 × 239 (11 ½ × 9 ⅜)
Collection: Katharine Y. Keck, Washington

92 SHAKESPEARE VISION, 1918
Crayon and pencil on paper
495 × 425 (19 ½ × 16 ¾)
Signed l.r.: W. Lehmbruck
Collection: Family of the Artist, Inv. No. 870

95 LARGE KNEELING WOMAN, 1911
P 13 I
349 × 250 (13 ½ × 9 ⅞)
Signed: l.r.: W. Lehmbruck

graphics

*The numbering of Lehmbruck's graphic
works is according to the catalog by Erwin
Petermann. All prints are from the
collection of the Lehmbruck family, unless
otherwise noted.*

96 THREE WOMEN, STANDING, 1912
P 22 II
196 × 150 (7 ¾ × 5 ⅞)
Estate Stamp

97 HEAD OF A WOMAN,
LARGE, 1912
P 24
295 × 260 (11 ⅝ × 10 ¼)
Signed l.r.: W. Lehmbruck

etchings

93 MOTHER AND CHILD (FULL
FIGURE, KNEELING), 1910
P 2 I
236 × 177 (9 ¼ × 7)
Signed l.r.: W. Lehmbruck

98 CRUCIFIXION, 1912
P 34 I
239 × 180 (9 ⅜ × 7 ⅛)
Signed l.r.: W. Lehmbruck

99 DEPRESSED WOMAN, 1912
P 37 II
200 × 245 (7 ⅞ × 9 ⅝)
Signed l.r.: W. Lehmbruck

100 MAN RISING, 1912/13
P 42 I
240 × 178 (9 ½ × 7)
Signed l.r.: W. Lehmbruck

101 FOUR WOMEN, 1913
P 56
295 × 195 (11 ⅝ × 7 ⅝)
Signed l.r.: W. Lehmbruck

102 GRIEVING WOMAN, 1913
P 57
410 × 240 (16 ⅛ × 9 ½)
Signed l.r.: W. Lehmbruck

103 JEREMIAH, 1913
P 61
240 × 180 (9 ½ × 7 ⅛)
Signed l.r.: W. Lehmbruck

104 SUSANNA, 1913
P 62 II
200 × 150 (7 ⅞ × 5 ⅞)
Signed l.r.: W. Lehmbruck

105 THE GREAT RESURRECTION, 1913
P 67
395 × 295 (15 ½ × 11 ⅝)
Signed: l.r. W. Lehmbruck

106 PAOLO AND FRANCESCA
(VERTICAL FORMAT), 1913
P 69 I
290 × 197 (11 ⅜ × 7 ¾)
Signed l.l.: W. Lehmbruck

107 RESURRECTION II, 1913
P 72 II
295 × 195 (11 ⅝ × 7 ⅝)
Signed l.r.: W. Lehmbruck

108 THE PRODIGAL SON, 1913
P 74 I
297 × 197 (11 ⅝ × 7 ¾)
Signed l.l.: W. Lehmbruck

109 RECLINING WOMAN, 1914
P 81 (not illustrated)
178 × 239 (6 ¹⁵⁄₁₆ × 9 ⁷⁄₁₆)
Collection: Katharine Y. Keck, Washington

110 VISION, 1914
P 84
178 × 237 (7 × 9 ¼)
Signed l.r.: W. Lehmbruck

111 THE DEAD MAN, 1914
P 86 II
238 × 180 (9 ⅜ × 7 ⅛)
Signed l.r.: W. Lehmbruck

112 WOMAN'S DREAM, 1914
P 94
337 × 239 (13 ¼ × 9 ⅜)
Signed l.r.: W. Lehmbruck

113 THE FLOOD, 1914
P 95 II
390 × 295 (15 ⅜ × 11 ⅝)
Signed l.r.: W. Lehmbruck

114 MEDEA, 1914
P 97 I
295 × 235 (11 ⅝ × 9 ¼)
Estate Stamp

115 MAN WALKING
(SMALL FORMAT), 1914
P 136
247 × 166 (9 ¾ × 6 ½)
Estate Stamp

116 MOTHER AND CHILD
(LARGE FORMAT), 1915
P 141
275 × 228 (10 ¾ × 9)
Signed l.r.: W. Lehmbruck

117 PORTRAIT OF A WOMAN VIII
(FRAU B), 1917
P 147
357 × 275 (14 × 10 ¾)
Signed l.r.: W. Lehmbruck

118 MAN AND WOMAN III, 1917
P 153
373 × 296 (14 ⅝ × 11 ⅝)
Estate Stamp

119   PIETÀ I, 1916/17
P 159
300 × 400 (11 ¾ × 15 ¾)
Estate Stamp

120   PIETÀ II, 1917
P 160
300 × 195 (11 ¾ × 7 ⅝)
Estate Stamp

121   WOUNDED GENIUS, 1917
P 163
300 × 195 (11 ¾ × 7 ⅝)
Estate Stamp

122   MACBETH I, 1918
P 178
400 × 297 (15 ¾ × 11 ⅝)
Estate Stamp

123   MACBETH II, 1918
P 179
400 × 300 (15 ¾ × 11 ¾)
Estate Stamp

124   MACBETH III, 1918
P 180
395 × 298 (15 ½ × 11 ¾)
Estate Stamp

125   MACBETH IV, 1918
P 181 II
395 × 298 (15 ½ × 11 ¾)
Estate Stamp

126   MACBETH V, 1918
P 182
395 × 295 (15 ½ × 11 ⅝)
Estate Stamp

lithographs

127   TWO WOUNDED MEN I
P L1
395 × 315 (15 ⁹⁄₁₆ × 12 ⅜)
Signed in the stone on r.: W. Lehmbruck

128   PORTRAIT OF THEODOR
DÄUBLER, 1916
P L3
282 × 193 (11 ⅛ × 7 ⁹⁄₁₆)
Signed in the stone, l.r.: Theodor Däubler,
W. Lehmbruck,
1916.
Signed l.r.: A. Lehmbruck

129 HEAD OF A WOMAN,
FRONTAL VIEW

P L6

335 × 220 (13 ¾₁₆ × 8 ⅝)

Signed in the stone, l.r.: W. Lehmbruck

Signed l.r.: A. Lehmbruck

130 MOTHER AND CHILD I

P L8

375 × 220 (14 ¾ × 8 ⅝)

Signed l.r.: A. Lehmbruck

Nature

And if knowledge and mankind

fill you with despair,

If recitation and oration

seem in vain,

Because it remains alien

to the truth in you,

Then come back to nature

and be her friend.

· · · ·

Wilhelm Lehmbruck, January, 1904

Figure of a standing man (now lost)

There are many who wish they too could give mankind a great, divine truth which would be a source of joy for centuries. But an aspect of egotism and pride appears in their belief that Christ, Savonarola, and Socrates died for the new truth, because death appeared as the only means of testifying to the truth before the mocking masses of mankind. The greater viewpoint, however, is the one that regards it as insignificant who the carrier of truth is, so long as the truth is communicated to a foundering humanity. Those people who believe that Christ or Socrates died for their teachings only to have a better life after death lower these divine exemplars to the level of egotism, even though it is the highest possible level of egotism. No, they died for the sake of truth itself and alone; in their boundless love they could act in no other way. And because all good generated by one person for others also becomes the focal point of pleasure, just as a light is only bright because all rays collect in it again. In this way, Christ and Savonarola had already called forth the heavenly pleasure of human salvation through their love and truth. All of heaven, all bliss concentrates itself in them, i.e. the heaven into which they yearn to bring mankind, the heaven in which everything flows toward a single goal: Love.

Wilhelm Lehmbruck

Lehmbruck Museum, Duisburg

Plates

Midnight

My hands plead stretched out in darkest night.
They rise and reach for darkness, for nothingness;
and yet, beyond the darkness there must be light. My
hands stretch out and plead and beg and tremble and
search, and they seek to find something in the dark-
ness, to hold and grasp it. And they grasp and feel
around and fail to find it, and all they grasp is
nothingness and darkness. And since they cannot
find anything, and since they cannot reach out to
brightness and light, they despair and grasp each
other and wrestle each other and hurt each
other and choke each other so as not to feel
the pains of the fever which causes them to
tremble. And despairingly, they fall in pain and
yearn to be buried away from pain. They sink them-
selves into my face and crush it. Here they find some-
thing to hold and surround and crush. It is something
quivering, hot, living, raging, burning; it answers
them and is not silent. With them it screams
and weeps in the darkness, and together
they hurl forth scalding words, like the
last hot scream of a prayer. And a flaming,
blood-red sparkling, star-hurling sheet of fire
races through the darkness and rages through
me and pulls me upward and back down
over the greatest heights and
fearful canyons and abysses.

And then night returns
and nothingness.

Wilhelm Lehmbruck

12 INCLINED HEAD
OF A WOMAN, 1910

18 TEMPTATION, 1911

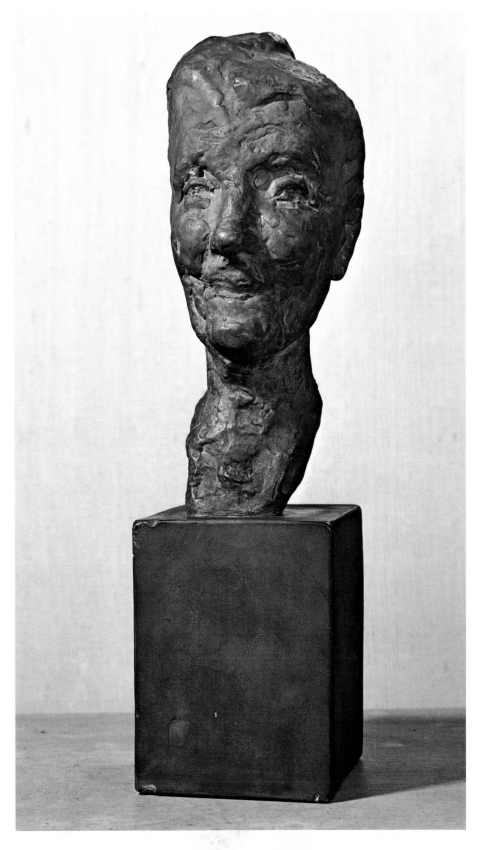

24   HEAD OF AN OLD WOMAN, 1913

27 RISING YOUTH, 1913

29 TORSO OF A GIRL LOOKING
OVER HER SHOULDER, 1913/14

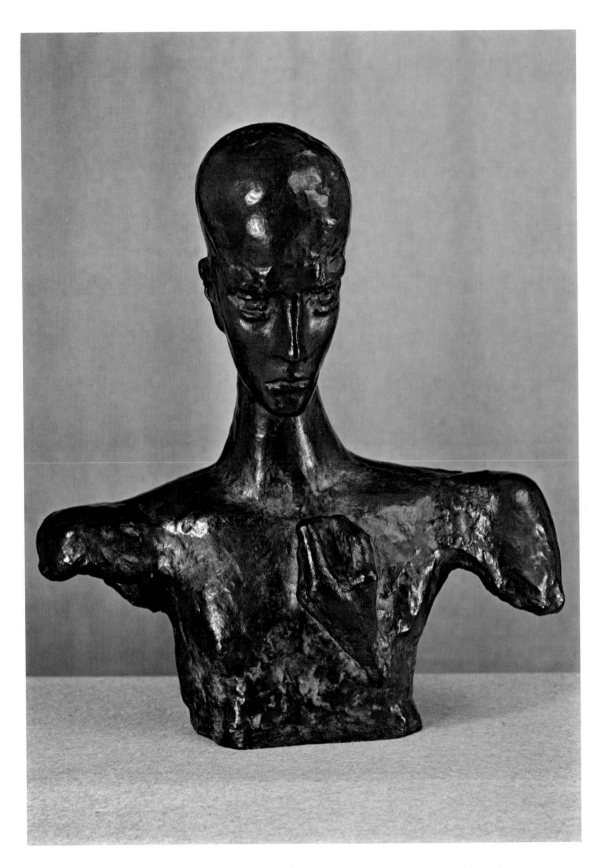

53 HEAD OF A THINKER, (1918)

59 ABDUCTION, 1913

75 FALLEN FEMALE NUDE, c. 1913/14

1 SELF-PORTRAIT, 1898

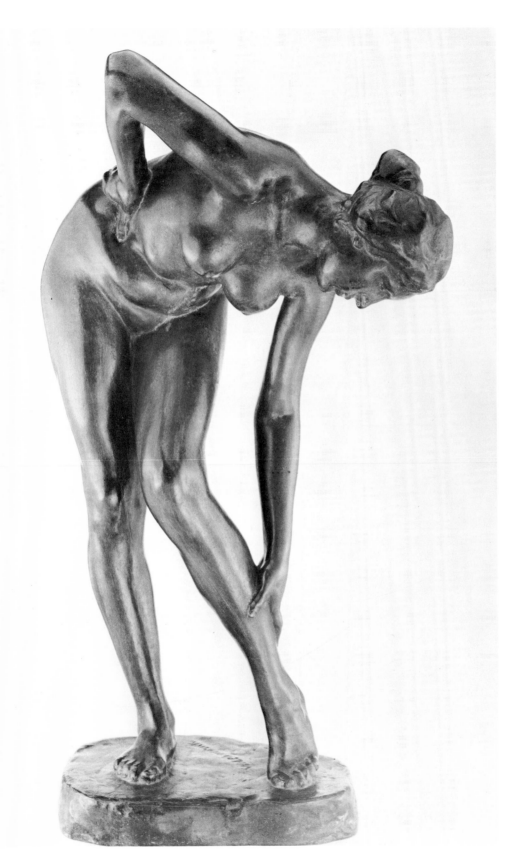

2   BATHING WOMAN, 1902

3   STONE-ROLLER ("WORK"),
     ca. 1903-1905?

4   THE MINER, ca. 1903-1905?

5   THE PATH TO BEAUTY:
PLAQUE HONORING
PROFESSOR SCHILL, 1905

6   MOTHER AND CHILD, 1907

7 MEDITATION: MOTHER
AND CHILD, 1907

8 FEMALE FIGURE II, 1908

9 GRIEVING WOMAN, 1909

10 STANDING FEMALE FIGURE, 1910

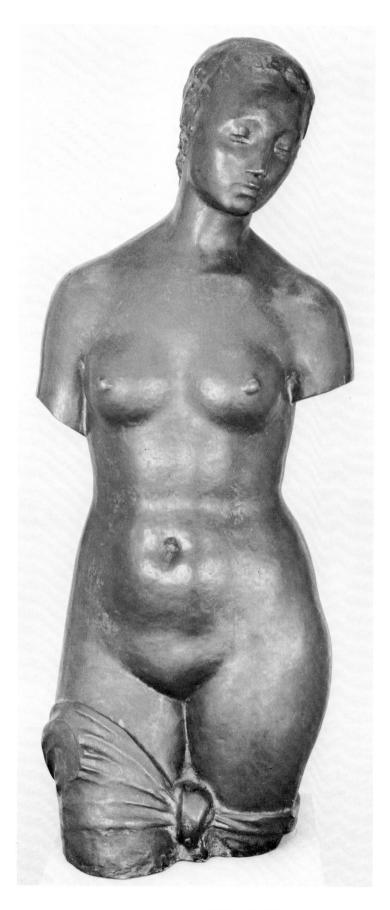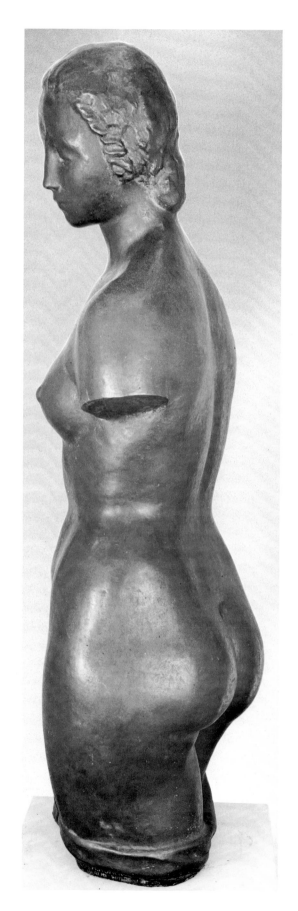

11   FEMALE TORSO, 1910

13　BUST OF FRAU LEHMBRUCK, 1910

14 PORTRAIT HEAD OF
FRAU LEHMBRUCK, 1910

15 GIRL RESTING, 1910

16 SEATED CHILD, 1910

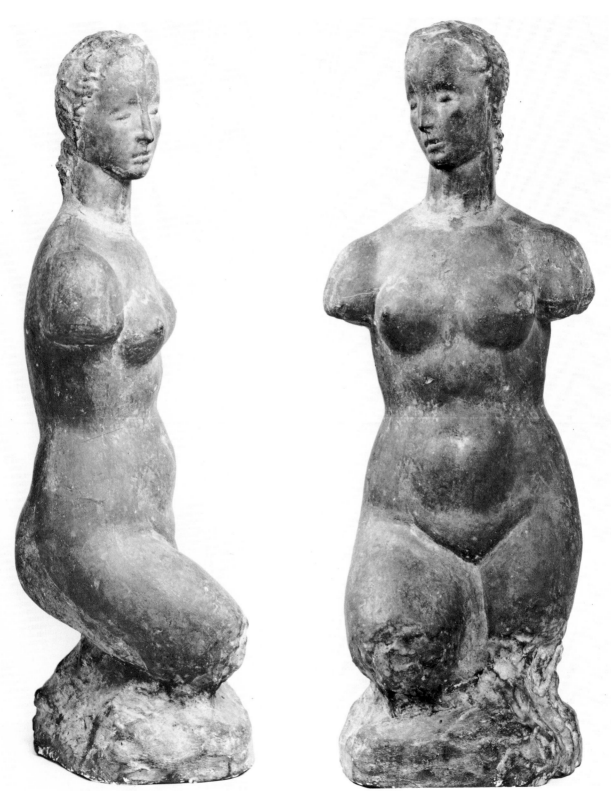

17   SMALL FEMALE TORSO, 1910/11

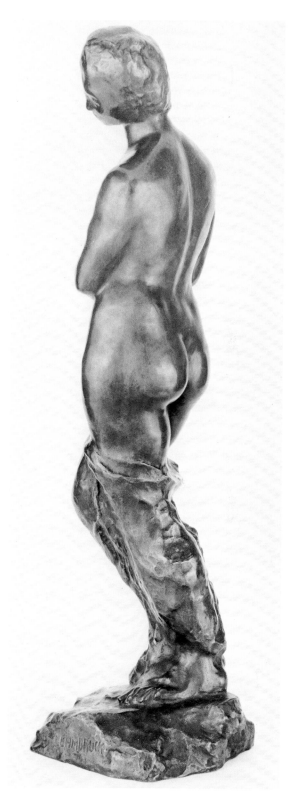

19 STATUETTE OF
A PENSIVE WOMAN, 1911

20 STATUETTE OF
A PENSIVE WOMAN, 1911

22   KNEELING WOMAN, 1911

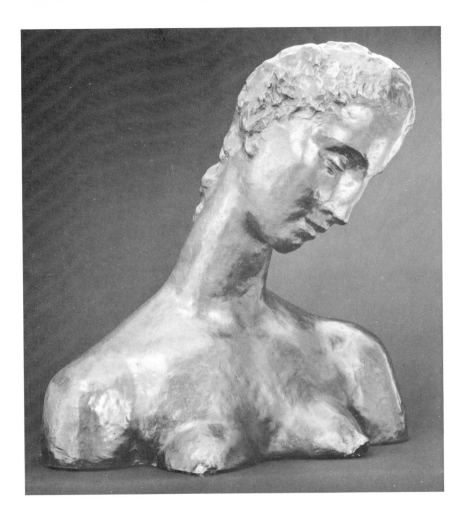

23 HEAD OF KNEELING
WOMAN, 1911

25   BOWING FEMALE TORSO, 1913

26 BOWING FEMALE TORSO, 1913

28 HEAD OF THE
RISING YOUTH, 1913

30 HEAD OF A GIRL LOOKING
OVER HER SHOULDER, 1913/14

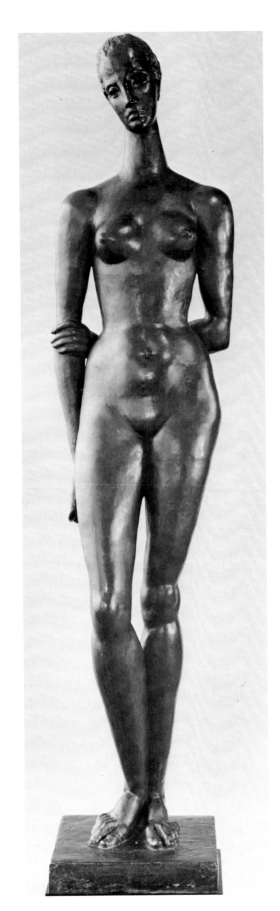

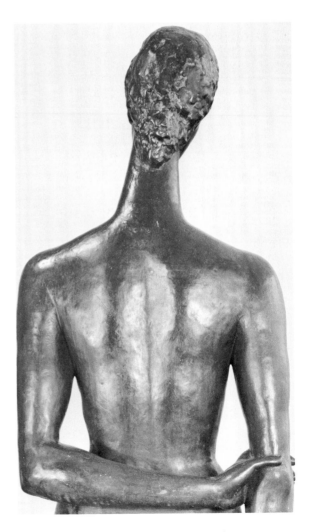

31 PENSIVE WOMAN, 1913/14

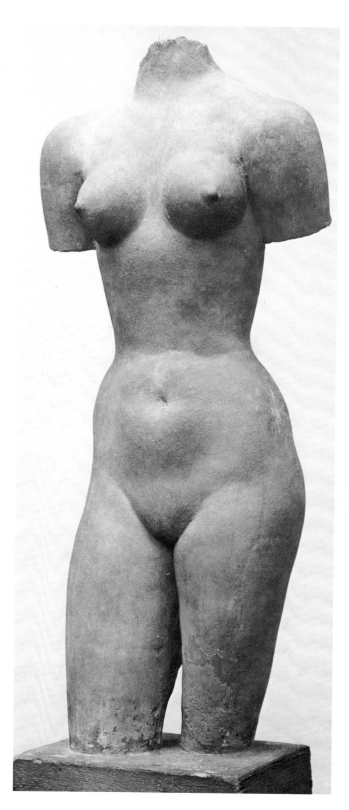

32 TORSO OF THE
    PENSIVE WOMAN, 1913/14

33 TORSO OF THE
    PENSIVE WOMAN, 1913/14

34 HEAD OF A WOMAN WITH
A SLENDER NECK, 1913/14

35 SEATED GIRL, 1913/14

36 BATHING GIRL, 1914

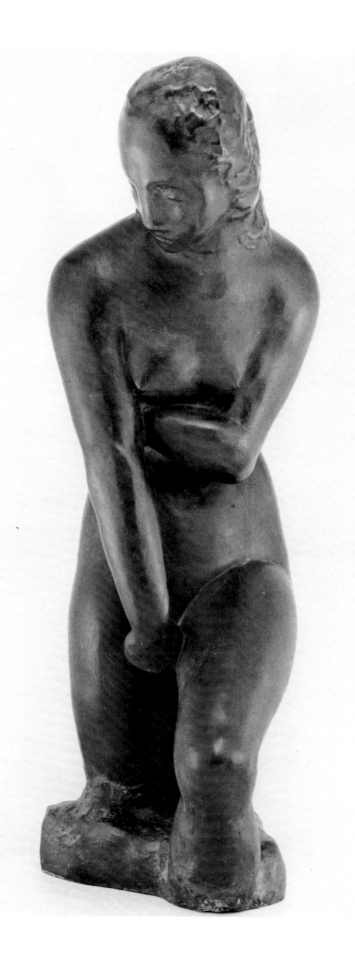

37 THREE WOMEN, RELIEF, 1914

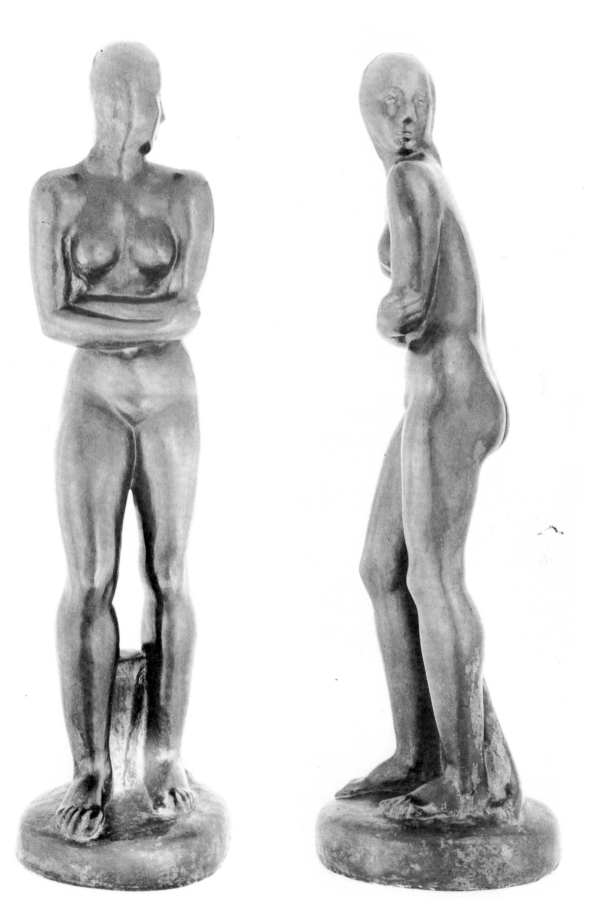

38 GIRL LOOKING OVER
HER SHOULDER, 1914/15

39 PORTRAIT OF
HERR FALK, 1915/16

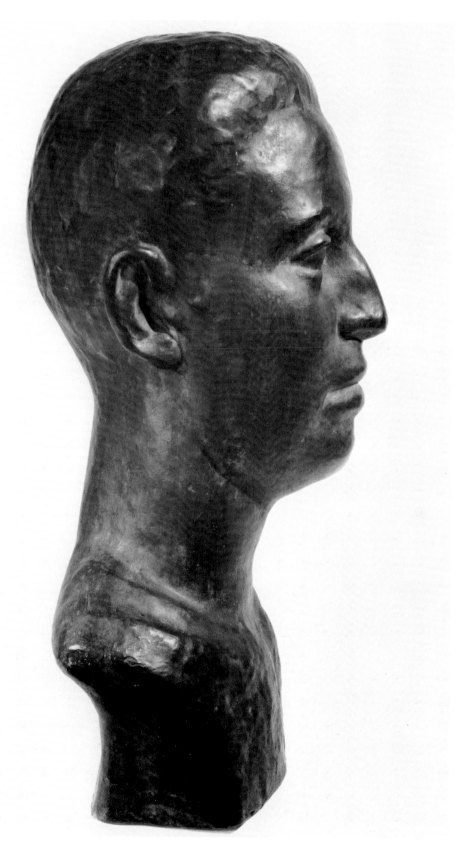

40 PORTRAIT OF
HERR FALK, 1915

41 PORTRAIT BUST OF
FRAU FALK, 1915/16

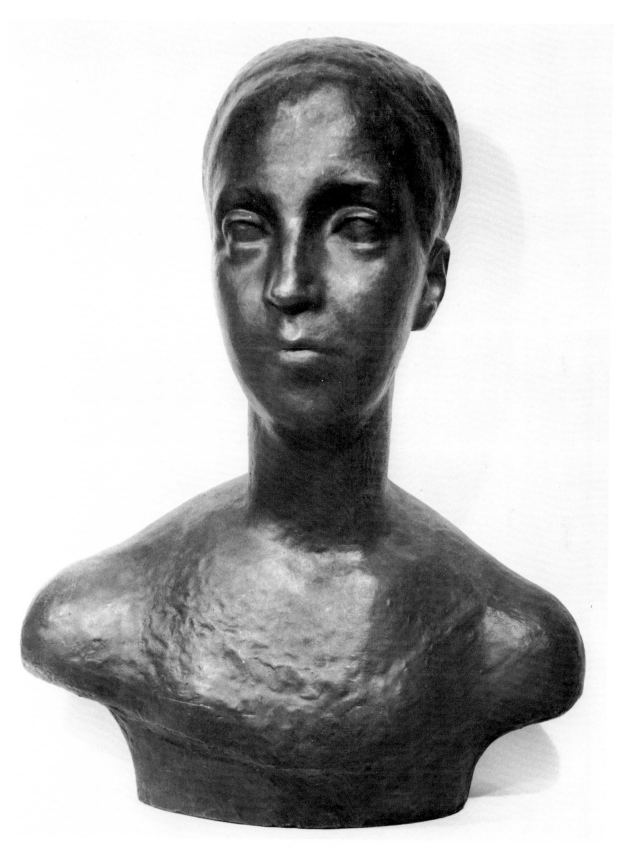

42 PORTRAIT BUST OF
FRAU FALK, 1915/16

43 PORTRAIT BUST OF
FRAU FALK, 1915/16

44 PORTRAIT STATUETTE OF
FRAU FALK, 1915/16

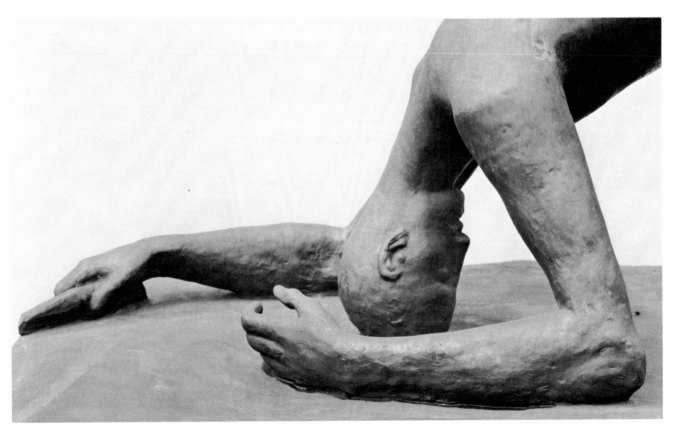

45 FALLEN MAN, 1915/16

46 PORTRAIT BUST OF
MISS K, 1916

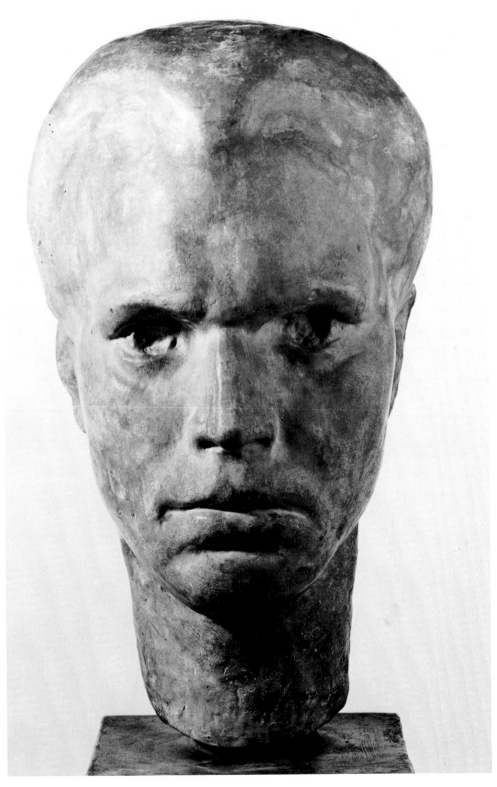

47   PORTRAIT OF FRITZ
VON UNRUH, 1917

49 PORTRAIT BUST OF MRS. B
(Version II), 1918

50   HEAD OF FRAU LEHMBRUCK, 1918

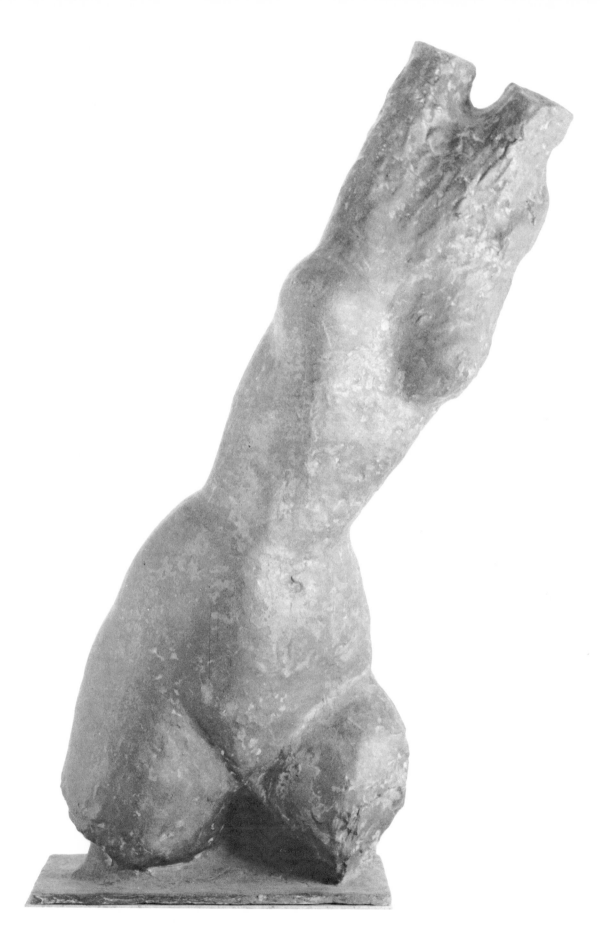

51 FEMALE TORSO
(FRAGMENT), 1918

52 MOTHER AND CHILD, 1918

54 LOVING HEADS, 1918

55 PRAYING GIRL, 1918

56 MARTHA, 1912

57 PORTRAIT OF A WOMAN, 1912

58 SUSANNA, 1913

60 PIETÀ, 1915

61 RECLINING FEMALE
NUDE, 1916

62 CROUCHING FEMALE
NUDE, 1917

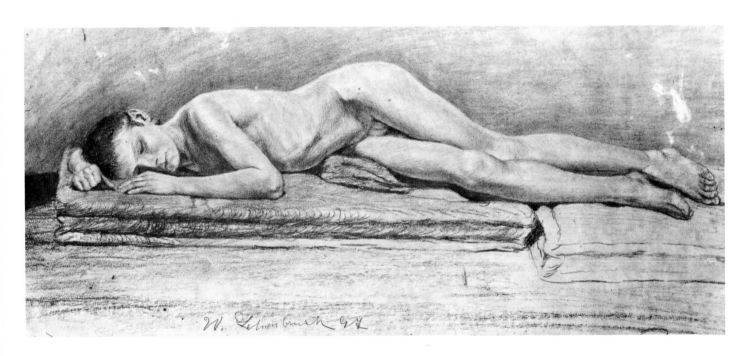

63 RECLINING BOY, 1897

64 DRAWINGS FOR RICHARD
DEHMEL'S DIE MAGD, c. 1902

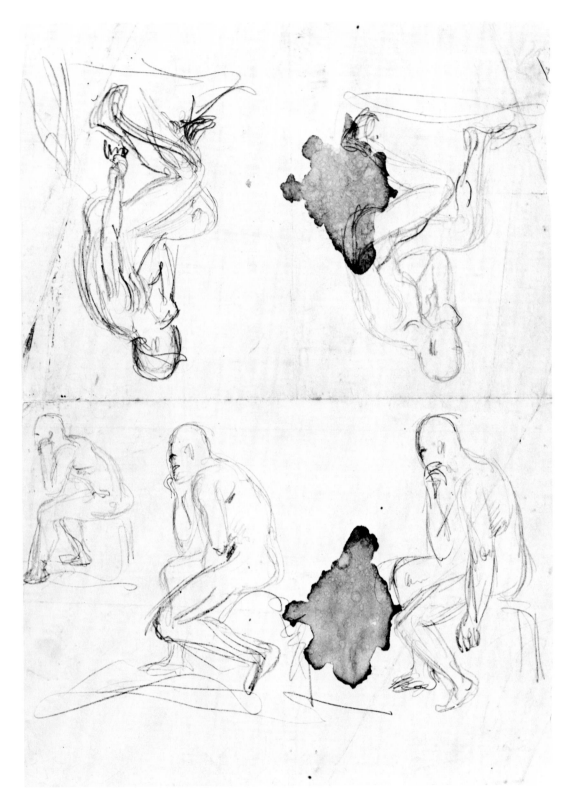

65 FIVE STUDIES FOR THE MINER, c. 1903-05?

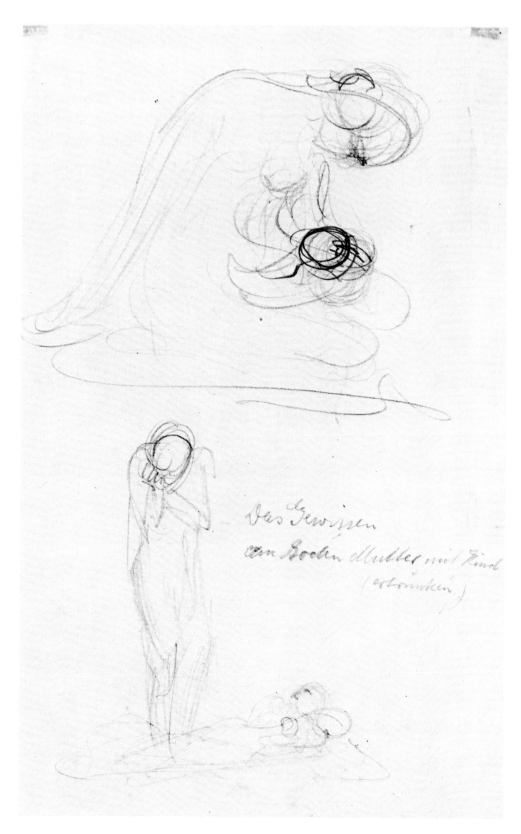

66 STUDY FOR MOTHER AND CHILD
AND PROJECT FOR A SCULPTURE:
CONSCIENCE: MOTHER WITH
DROWNED CHILD, c. 1905-06?

67 SEATED CHILD, 1911

68 SKETCH FOR KNEELING WOMAN, 1911

69 STANDING FEMALE NUDE
WITH DRAPERY, c. 1910-12?

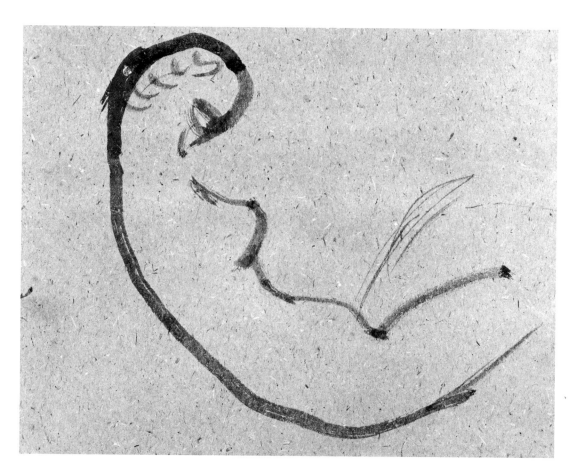

70 RECLINING NUDE, 1913

71 SEATED GIRL, 1913

72 PENSIVE YOUTH, 1913

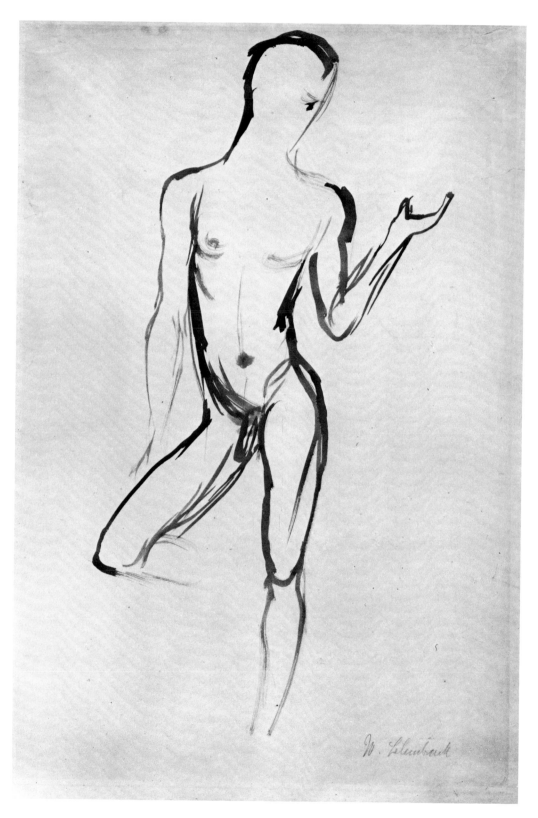

73 MALE NUDE, c. 1913

74 THREE FIGURES, 1913

76 FEMALE NUDE WITH
ARMS FOLDED, 1914

77   SKETCH FOR FALLEN MAN, 1915

78 WOUNDED WARRIOR, c. 1915

79   SKETCHES: THE YOUNG
REGIMENTS AND
THE LAST CRY, 1916

80 SKETCH FOR FALLEN
MAN, c. 1916

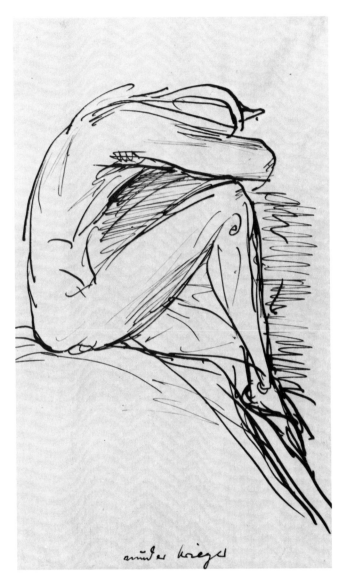

81   EXHAUSTED WARRIOR, 1916

82 AWAKENING WARRIOR
(RESURRECTION), 1916

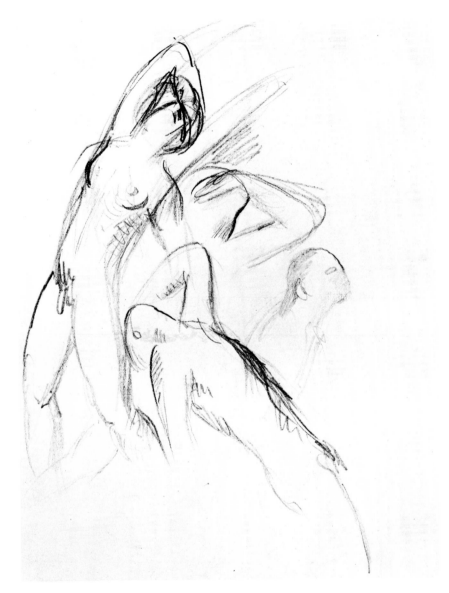

83 FOUR CHARGING,
WOUNDED WARRIORS, 1916

84　CONTEMPORARY PIETÀ, 1916

85 PORTRAIT OF THEODOR
DÄUBLER, 1916/17

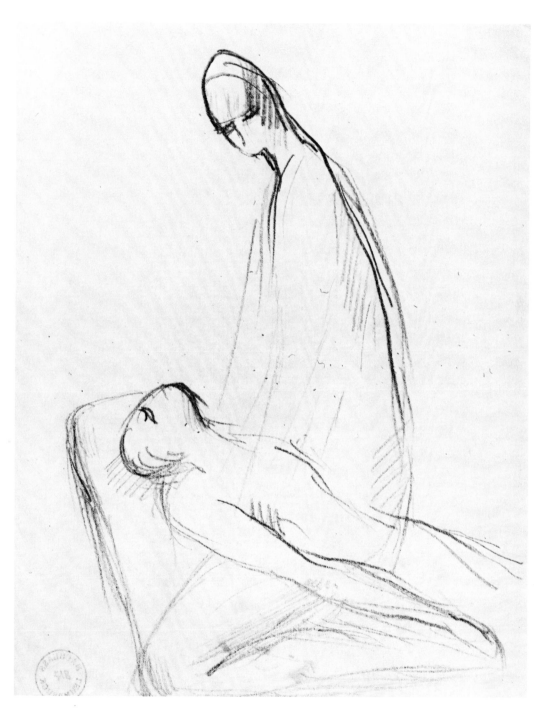

86 PIETÀ, 1917/18

87 PIETÀ, 1917/18

88 PIETÀ, 1917/18

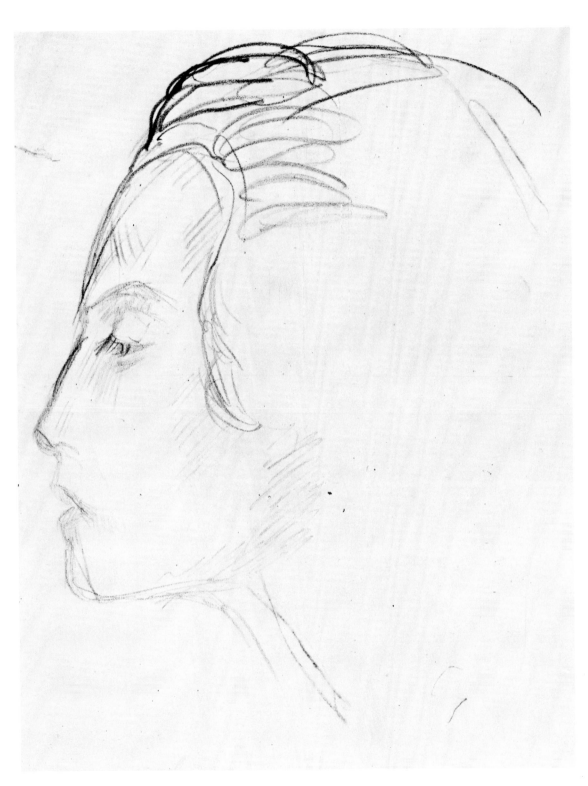

89 HEAD OF A WOMAN,
PROFILE, 1918

90 HEAD OF A WOMAN, 1918

91 SKETCH FOR LOVING HEADS
(LIPS CRADLED ON ARM), 1918

92 SHAKESPEARE VISION, 1918

93 MOTHER AND CHILD (FULL FIGURE, KNEELING), 1910

95   LARGE KNEELING WOMAN, 1911

96   THREE WOMEN, STANDING, 1912

97 HEAD OF A WOMAN,
LARGE, 1912

98 CRUCIFIXION, 1912

99   DEPRESSED WOMAN, 1912

100 MAN RISING, 1912/13

101 FOUR WOMEN, 1913

102   GRIEVING WOMAN, 1913

103   JEREMIAH, 1913   104   SUSANNA, 1913

105 THE GREAT RESURRECTION, 1913

106 PAOLO AND FRANCESCA
(VERTICAL FORMAT), 1913

107 RESURRECTION II, 1913

108 THE PRODIGAL SON, 1913

110   VISION, 1914

111 THE DEAD MAN, 1914

112 WOMAN'S DREAM, 1914

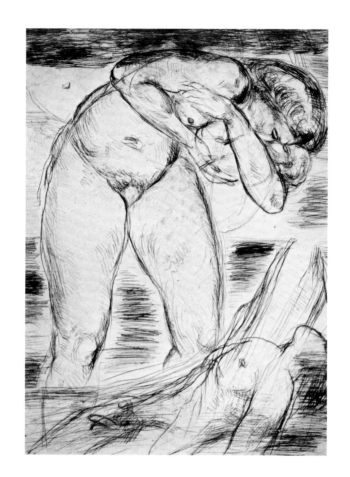

113   THE FLOOD, 1914

114   MEDEA, 1914

115 MAN WALKING
(SMALL FORMAT), 1914

116 MOTHER AND CHILD
(LARGE FORMAT), 1915

117 PORTRAIT OF A WOMAN VIII
     (FRAU B), 1917

118 MAN AND WOMAN III, 1917

119 PIETÀ I, 1916/17

120   PIETÀ II, 1917

121   WOUNDED GENIUS, 1917

122 MACBETH I, 1918

123 MACBETH II, 1918

124 MACBETH III, 1918

125   MACBETH IV, 1918

126   MACBETH V, 1918

127 TWO WOUNDED MEN I

128   PORTRAIT OF THEODOR
DÄUBLER, 1916

129   HEAD OF A WOMAN,
FRONTAL VIEW

130   MOTHER AND CHILD I

Appendices

biographical notes

This account of the artist's life and exhibitions is based on monographs by Paul Westheim and August Hoff supplemented and corrected with unpublished material from the archives of the Wilhelm Lehmbruck Museum, Duisburg, and of Mr. Guido Lehmbruck, Stuttgart.

1881   Born January 4 at Huhnerorter Strasse 4 in Meiderich, a small German mining town now incorporated into the city of Duisburg. Son of Wilhelm Lehmbruck, a miner, and Margareta Lehmbruck, née Wützmann. Both parents were descended from Westphalian farming families.

February 6, is baptized into the Lutheran faith and receives the name Heinrich Wilhelm.

1895   March 22, (age 14) graduates from the Meiderich *Volksschule*. His final evaluation reads:

Behavior: good
Ambition: good
Attention: good
Attendance: regular
Religion: very good
German:
    Reading: very good
    Composition: very good
    Penmanship: good
Mathematics: very good
Spatial science: very good

About this time begins carving small plaster figures, mostly portraits and copies of monuments to German national heroes which he finds illustrated in textbooks.

Summer: Enters the School of Arts and Crafts in Düsseldorf. His expenses for the academic year are paid by one of his teachers from Meiderich, G. von Diepenbrock.

1896   Receives a small fellowship from the community of Meiderich.

1899   His father dies. To obtain money for himself and the family, draws anatomical and botanical studies as textbook illustrations. Active as an assistant in various sculpture ateliers in Düsseldorf.

1901   May, enters the Düsseldorf Academy of Art and studies with Karl Janssen. Becomes a "Master Student" and thereby receives free materials, studio space and models. Creates large, academic nudes as well as projects for monuments to mythological heroes.

1902   The Düsseldorf Academy obtains his *Bathing Woman* for its collection of students' work.

1904   At the Düsseldorf International Exhibition (May 1–October 23) sees a large retrospective exhibition of 60 works by Auguste Rodin.

July 5, writes a poem on the motif of Rodin's *Kiss*. At the exhibition, also sees works by Jules Dalou, Albert Bartholomé, Constantin Meunier and Jef Lambeaux. Travels to Holland and England.

1905   August. Enters into contract with the Düsseldorf art dealer Bismeyer and Kraus to make a small scale model of Düsseldorf's civic trademark, Grupello's equestrian monument to Jan Wellem (1711). The souvenir statuette, sold for 300 and 450 marks, was exhibited at Schulte's Art Salon in Cologne.

By way of Munich, travels to Italy (Milan, Genoa, Pisa, Florence, Rome, Naples and Capri). Makes numerous drawings, notably of Roman sculpture, Michelangelo's Medici Chapel and genre scenes of Italian life.

1906   Lives at Florastrasse 4, Düsseldorf.
December, leaves the Düsseldorf Academy.

1907   Joins the Association of Düsseldorf Artists and the Société Nationale des Beaux-Arts. Travels to Paris and exhibits there for the first time.

1908   Brief journey to Paris.
June 6, marries Anita Kaufmann (b. February 24, 1879–d. July 9, 1961).

1909   The colossal figure *Man* (c. 10 feet high, destroyed) demonstrates close dependence on Michelangelo and Rodin.

March 11, his first son, Gustav Wilhelm is born in Düsseldorf.

1910   Moves to Paris with his family. Lives on Montparnasse, Rue de Vaugigard 105.

Frequents the Café du Dôme where the German students of the Académie Matisse meet. Befriends Archipenko and comes into contact with Brancusi, Dunoyer de Segonzac, Derain, Le Fauconnier, Léger and Modigliani. Begins work in graphics and is introduced to the process of stone casting. Visits Rodin's atelier but breaks away from his influence, as demonstrated by the *Standing Woman*.

1911 Moves to Avenue du Main 127, Paris. The *Kneeling Woman* demonstrates a major stylistic shift in his work.

1912 In a letter dated January 9, is invited by Fritz Mackensen to join the faculty of the Saxon Academy of Fine Arts in Weimar. Apparently rejects this offer. April, second trip to Italy financed through an advance of 2,250 marks received from the Duisburg Museum Association, in commission for a marble version of the *Standing Woman*.

Trip to Berlin.

September. Attends the Cologne Sonderbund Exhibition. Meets the American painter Walt Kuhn and is invited to participate in the New York Armory Show.

1913 In Paris.

March. At the Armory Show in New York City, the stone cast of the *Standing Woman* is sold for $1620; six etchings are sold for $81.

June 13. His son Manfred is born in Paris.

Commissioned to create two figures for the Cologne Werkbund Exhibition.

1914 June 22, notification from Arthur B. Davies of an insurance payment of 5,000 francs for damage suffered by the *Kneeling Woman* during transport from Boston to New York.

July, with the threat of war flees Paris with his family.

August 1, arrives in Duisburg-Meiderich where he is registered with the military reserve. His family stays in Cologne, Neue Mastrichter Strasse 26.

November 17, moves to Berlin with his family. Lives briefly at Wilhelmshöherstrasse 5, then at Rübenstrasse 26 in Berlin-Schöneberg.

December 8, sets up his studio at Fehlerstrasse 1, Berlin-Friedenau, near the bronze foundry of Hermann Noack.

1915 Moves to Uhlandstrasse 76, Berlin-Wilmersdorf.

March, to meet qualifications for medical duty in the military takes ambulance driving lessons. Continues attempts to avoid being classified for active military duty.

October 27, moves to Südwestchause 4, Berlin-Friedenau.

December 15, receives notification of his military activation as a battle painter and is ordered to report for duty at Strassburg. Begins friendship with the Falk family.

1916 February 16, receives notification of a change of his military classification to Inactive Member of the Medical Corps. Seeks to leave Germany for Switzerland to escape military duty. Moves his family into a studio on the Fehlerstrasse.

November 16, Max Liebermann recommends that Lehmbruck be permitted to work and exhibit in Switzerland for the purpose of increasing "there the understanding of what German artists are seeking to do."

November 17, in Frankfurt with Julius Meier-Graefe on the way to Mannheim.

December 2, arrives in Zurich, Switzerland; stays at the Savoy Hotel.

1917 Living in Zurich, Dufourstrasse 48.

January 9, telegrams his family in Berlin to accompany the Falk family to Zurich immediately, and to send his sculptures to the Zurich Kunsthaus.

Receives medical certification of periodic states of great depression.

February 2, his son Guido is born.

Befriends the actress Elisabeth Bergner.

Limited contacts with the artists Carl Hofer, Hermann Hubacher, and Julius Schwyzer.

Creates portrait head of dramatist Fritz von Unruh.

Completes the *Seated Youth*.

1918 Moves to Höhenweg 8, Zurich.

Constant travel between Berlin and Zurich.

1919 January 24, selected a member of the Prussian Academy of Fine Arts along with Lovis Corinth, Georg Kolbe, Franz Metzner, Käthe Kollwitz and Ernst Barlach.

C. mid-March, arrives without his family in Berlin.

March 19, letter of official notification of his selection to the Prussian Academy of Fine Arts is sent to his Zurich address.

Writes his wife of his renewed will to live and create and promises a better future.

March 25, commits suicide.

April 2, burial at the Cemetery of the Twelve Apostles, Berlin-Schöneberg. The poet Hans Bethge delivers the funeral oration.

exhibitions 1906-1918

1906   May 5–October 10. Cologne, German Art Exhibition (1 sculpture)

1907   April 14–June 30. Paris, Salon de la Société Nationale des Beaux-Arts. (4 sculptures)

May 11–September 29. Düsseldorf, Exhibition of German National Art. (4 sculptures)

June 4–July 28. Düsseldorf, Association of Düsseldorf Artists. (3 sculptures)

December 11–January 11, 1908. Essen, City Museum, Exhibition of works by Friedrich Kalmorgen and Wilhelm Lehmbruck. (3 sculptures)

1908   April 15–June 30. Paris, Salon de la Société Nationale des Beaux-Arts. (2 sculptures)

June 1–October. Munich, Annual Exhibition in the Glaspalast. (3 sculptures)

June 7–?. Düsseldorf, Exhibition of the Artists' Association for the Rhineland and Westphalia. (2 sculptures)

(?). Cologne, Kunstverein. (2 sculptures)

1909   April 15–June 30. Paris, Salon de la Société Nationale des Beaux-Arts. (2 sculptures)

May 1–September 26. Berlin, Great Annual Berlin Art Exhibition. (2 sculptures)

May 15–October 10. Düsseldorf, Great Art Exhibition of the Society for the Propagation of Art Exhibitions. (1 sculpture)

May 15–October 10. Düsseldorf, Exhibition of Christian Art. (9 sculptures)

June ?. Düsseldorf, Exhibition of the Artists' Association for the Rhineland and Westphalia. (1 sculpture)

1910   April 15–June 30. Paris, Salon de la Société Nationale des Beaux-Arts. (3 sculptures)

October 1–November 8. Paris, Salon d'Automne. (3 sculptures, 1 painting, 1 drawing)

1911   April 15–June 30. Paris, Salon de la Société Nationale des Beaux-Arts. (2 sculptures)

April 24–June 13. Paris, Salon des Indépendant. (3 sculptures, 2 paintings)

May 15–October 31. Munich, International Exhibition of the Munich Secession. (2 sculptures)

May 27–October 8. Düsseldorf, Great Art Exhibition. (2 sculptures)

October 1–November 8. Paris, Salon d'Automne. (5 sculptures, 5 pastels)

1912   March 20–May 16. Paris, Salon des Indépendants. (2 sculptures, 17 prints)

April 1–?. Hagen, Museum Folkwang. (5 sculptures, 5 paintings, 2 pastels, prints)

(?). Berlin, Twenty-fourth Exhibition of the Secession. (2 sculptures)

May 15–September 30. Cologne, Sonderbund Exhibition. (5 sculptures, 2 paintings)

November–December. Berlin, Twenty-fifth Exhibition of the Secession. (1 pastel, 5 prints)

1913   January. Cologne, Annual Exhibition of the Cologne Secession. (1 sculpture, 3 pastels, 10 prints)

February 17–March 3. New York, The Armory Show (2 sculptures, 6 prints)

March 15–October 31. Baden-Baden, German Art Exhibition. (3 sculptures, 7 prints)

March 24–April 16. Chicago, The Armory Show. (2 sculptures)

April 24–May 14. Boston, The Armory Show. (1 sculpture)

May ?. Berlin, Twenty-sixth Exhibition of the Secession. (1 sculpture)

May 4–September 30. Mannheim, Society of German Artists. (5 sculptures)

October–November. Cologne, Kunstverein. (1 sculpture)

November 15–January 5, 1914. Paris, Salon d'Automne. (3 sculptures, 15 prints)

December 21–?. Düsseldorf, Galerie Flechtheim; Contributions to the Art of the 19th Century and of our Time. (2 sculptures)

1914   March 14–October 3. Baden-Baden, German Art Exhibition (1 sculpture)

April 12–end September. Berlin, First Exhibition of the Free Secession (3 sculptures)

May 1–July 31. Mannheim, Kunsthalle: Drawings and Sculptures of Modern

Sculptors. (4 sculptures, 15 drawings and prints)

May–October. Cologne, Werkbund Exhibition (2 sculptures)

May 30–October 1. Munich, First Exhibition of the New Munich Secession. (2 sculptures)

June 20–June 30. Paris, Galérie Levesque: Exhibition of the Work of Wilhelm Lehmbruck. (18 sculptures, 8 paintings, 40 prints)

1915 (?). Munich, First Spring Exhibition of the New Munich Secession (3 sculptures, 2 paintings, 9 prints)

1916 **February 5–April 5.** Berlin, Second Exhibition of the Free Secession. (4 sculptures, 2 paintings)

Mid-February–end of March. Cologne, Artists' Association: Art in Cologne's Private Collections. (2 sculptures)

(?). Berlin, Free Secession. (3 sculptures, drawings, and prints)

(?). Munich, New Secession. (2 sculptures, drawings, and prints)

November 12–December 6. Mannheim, Kunsthalle: Collective Exhibition of the Works of Wilhelm Lehmbruck. (25 sculptures, 10 paintings, drawings and prints)

1917 **February 1–April 1.** Wiesbaden, New Museum. The Kirchhoff Collection. (1 painting)

February 4–March 4. Zurich, Kunsthaus. (6 sculptures, drawings and prints)

July 1–September 30. Berlin, Third Exhibition of the Free Secession. (1 sculpture)

October 9–October 30. Basel, Kunsthalle: Exhibition Hodler-Lehmbruck-Stoecklin. (15 sculptures, 1 pastel, drawings and graphics)

1918 **May 18–October 18.** Darmstadt, Art Building on the Mathildenhöhe: German Art (1 sculpture, 1 painting, 3 prints)

(?). Berlin, Fourth Exhibition of the Free Secession. (2 sculptures)

(?). Munich, Fourth Exhibition of the New Secession. (1 sculpture, 19 prints)

exhibitions 1919-1971

Only one-man exhibitions or those in which a significant portion of the works exhibited were by Lehmbruck are listed. Excluded are auction or sales exhibitions as well as permanent museum exhibitions. Unless otherwise indicated, the exhibitions are devoted solely to Lehmbruck's work.

1919 **May–June.** Zurich, Kunstsalon Neupert: Lehmbruck Memorial Exhibition.

May–July. Berlin, Academy of Fine Arts. Spring Exhibition.

May–July. Berlin, Free Secession: Summer Exhibition with Memorial Exhibitions to Theo von Bruckhausen and Wilhelm Lehmbruck.

June 22–July 30. Düsseldorf, Kunsthalle: Das junge Rheinland.

July 27–August 16. Düsseldorf, Galerie Flechtheim: Paths to the Art of Today.

August 24–September 21. Bern, Kunsthalle: Exhibition Hodler-Fiori-Lehmbruck-Haller-Hubacher-Morgenthaler.

1920 **February.** Berlin, Galerie Paul Cassirer. Wilhelm Lehmbruck Memorial Exhibition.

May 15–October 3. Düsseldorf, Great Art Exhibition.

June 10–September 30. Darmstadt, Mathildenhöhe: German Expressionism.

1921 Munich, New Secession. Lehmbruck Memorial Exhibition.

January–February. Hamburg: Hansa Werkstätten: Lehmbruck Memorial Exhibition.

February–May. Stuttgart, Kunsthaus Schaller: Lehmbruck Memorial Exhibition.

May. Heilbronn, Kunstverein: Lehmbruck Memorial Exhibition.

July. Halberstadt, Kunstverein: Lehmbruck Memorial Exhibition.

1925 Duisburg, Museumsverein: Third Millenium Exhibition. Krefeld, Kaiser Wilhelm Museum.

Cologne, Kunstverein.

1927 Münster, Westfälischer Kunstverein.

1929 Berlin, Galerie Ferdinand Müller. Duisburg, Museumsverein.

1930 New York, Museum of Modern
Art: Lehmbruck-Maillol.

1936 Berlin, Galerie Nierendorf.

1939 New York, Marie Harriman Gallery.
New York, Museum of Modern Art:
Art in Our Time.

1941 Philadelphia, Museum of Art; Richmond,
Virginia Museum of Fine Arts:
Collection of Walter P. Chrysler, Jr.

1948 Tübingen, Kunstgebäude.
Bern, Kunsthalle.

1949 Mannheim, Kunsthalle.
Düsseldorf, Städtisches Kunstmuseum.
Hamburg, Kunsthalle.
Stuttgart, Staatsgalerie.

1951 New York, Curt Valentin Gallery.

1952 Washington, Corcoran Gallery:
Privately owned works from
the Washington area.

1953 Ulm, Städtisches Museum.
New York, Curt Valentin Gallery:
Sculpture and Sculptors' Drawings.

1955 Hannover, Kestner Gesellschaft.
Duisburg, Städtische Kunstsammlung.

1956 Bremen, Kunsthalle.
Bielefeld, Städtisches Kunsthaus.
Amsterdam, Stedelijk Museum.
Lübeck, Overbeck-Gesellschaft.
Zurich, Kunsthaus.

1957 London, Tate Gallery. Leeds, City Gallery.
Berlin, Haus am Waldsee.

New York, Museum of Modern Art,
St. Louis, City Art Museum:
German Art of the Twentieth Century.
New York, Knoedler & Co.; Cambridge,
Mass., Fogg Art Museum: Modern
Paintings, Drawings and Sculpture
from the Louise and Joseph Pulitzer, Jr.
Collection.

1961 Frankfurt, Kunstverein and
Kuratorium Kulturelles Frankfurt.
Antwerp, Koninklijke Academie
voor Schone Kunsten.
New York, Knoedler & Co.:
The James Thrall Soby Collection.

1962 Munich, Haus der Kunst.

1963 Vienna, Museum des 20. Jahrhunderts.
New York, Otto Gerson Gallery:
Lehmbruck and Other
German Sculptors of his Time.
New York, Marlborough-Gerson Gallery:
Artist and Maecenas:
A Tribute to Curt Valentin.

1964 Cassel, Documenta III.
Duisburg, Wilhelm Lehmbruck Museum:
Inaugural Exhibition.

1966 Berlin (East), State Museums:
19th and 20th Century German Art.

1969 Duisburg, Wilhelm Lehmbruck Museum:
Lehmbruck's Early Works.
New York, Museum of Modern Art:
Twentieth-Century Art from the
Nelson A. Rockefeller Collection.

1970 Zurich, ITH: Lehmbruck Graphics.

1971 Warsaw, National Museum:
Lehmbruck Graphics.

Effusion and Dreams

Place flowered wreaths on my hair, woven in triumph.
I dreamed of wreaths—
There exist wreaths, dark ones, heavy ones,
Glowing in rapture, drunken in scent.
There exist wreaths shining in purple,
Rose red, perfumed,
Appearing darkly from chalices, foam, and aglow
With sated colors and musty smells;
Red as blood pouring hot from a wound,
Hot as the mouth of love.
Shining suns are sucked into chalices,
Sparkling like rubies and wine,
Like the blood of suns before the darkest night.
Was it a wreath like this?
— I don't know.—
There exist wreaths, fresh with blossoms,
Like pearls, filled with silent sighs,
Pure as the silence of starshine,
Like spring snows in the morning warmth.

No. These weren't my wreaths.
There exist wreaths, gray ones, pale ones,
Exhausted from pain, in need of love,
Blown away from a flowering meadow,
Silently surrounded by accepting death,
Pale as Death.—

There exist wreaths, gray ones, frightened ones,
Without light, without blossoms,
For me—a wreath?

Wilhelm Lehmbruck

bibliography Compiled by Reinhold Heller & Margarita Kroczek

This bibliography is a listing of the critical and biographical information on Lehmbruck published since 1906. With few exceptions, newspaper reviews published after 1920 are omitted as are exhibition catalogs unless they contain significant contributions; likewise omitted are general studies in which Lehmbruck receives brief consideration.

Lehmbruck bibliographies have previously been compiled by Will Grohmann (bibl. 66), August Hoff (bibl. 5) and in the catalog of the Lehmbruck Exhibition held at the Kunsthalle Mannheim in 1949. Although still not complete, the present bibliography is far more exhaustive than these. The bibliography is divided into three sections: A. monographs on Wilhelm Lehmbruck, B. articles devoted specifically to Lehmbruck or his work, and C. articles and books in which Lehmbruck receives significant attention. The arrangement of the bibliography is alphabetical by the author's name or names, or by title in the case of unsigned articles.

Abbreviations used: *bibl.* this bibliography, [n.d.] not dated, [　] title supplied by compilers.

monographs

1. BETHGE, Hans. *Wilhelm Lehmbruck zum Gedächtnis*. Berlin-Wilmersdorf: Alfred Richard Meyer, 1920. Funeral oration and poem "Auf einen Mädchenkopf": See also bibl. 24, 25.

2. EINSTEIN, Carl. *Wilhelm Lehmbrucks graphisches Werk*. Berlin: Paul Cassirer, 1913. Essay accompanying a catalog of graphics printed by Cassirer.

3. HOFF, August. *Wilhelm Lehmbruck*. Berlin: Klinkhardt and Biermann, 1933. (*Junge Kunst*, Vol. 61/62) 20 p., 49 ill.

4. HOFF, August. *Wilhelm Lehmbruck, seine Sendung und sein Werk*. Berlin: Rembrandt-Verlag, 1936. 117 p., 90 ill. Includes oeuvre catalog.

5. HOFF, August. *Wilhelm Lehmbruck, Leben und Werk*. Berlin: Rembrandt-Verlag, 1961. (*Die Kunst aller Zeiten*, Vol. 13) 167 p., 120 ill. Revised and expanded edition of bibl. 4. Includes oeuvre catalog and extensive bibliography.

5a. HOFF, August. *Wilhelm Lehmbruck*. New York: Praeger, 1969. English translation of bibl. 5 without bibliography or oeuvre catalog. 159 p., 120 ill.

6. HOFMANN, Werner. *Wilhelm Lehmbruck*. Cologne: Kiepenheuer and Witsch, 1957 (Europäische Bildhauer). 17 p., 33 ill. 2nd ed. Munich and Ahrbeck: Knorr and Hirth, 1964.

6a. Editions in Dutch and in English of this same monograph. Amsterdam: A. de Lange, 1957. London: A. Zwemmer Ltd., 1958, and New York, 1959.

7. PETERMANN, Erwin. *Die Druckgraphik von Wilhelm Lehmbruck: Verzeichnis*. Stuttgart: Verlag Gerd Hatje, 1964. 37 p. introductory text, over 200 ill. Definitive catalog of Lehmbruck's prints. Each print is reproduced.

8. SALZMANN, Siegfried. *"Hinweg mit der 'Knienden'." ein Beitrag zur Geschichte des Kunstskandals*. Duisburg: Museumsverein Duisburg [n.d.] 19 p., 7 ill.

9. TRIER, Eduard. *Wilhelm Lehmbruck, Zeichnungen und Radierungen*. Munich: R. Piper & Co., 1955. (Piper-Bücherei, Vol. 84).

10. TRIER, Eduard. *Wilhelm Lehmbruck: Die Kniende*. Stuttgart: Reclam-Verlag, 1958. (Werkmonographien zur bildenden Kunst in Reclams Universal-Bibliothek, No. 32). Analysis of *The Kneeling Woman* with excerpts from bibl. 3, 11, 46, 291.

11. WESTHEIM, Paul. *Wilhelm Lehmbruck*. Potsdam: Gustav Kiepenheuer Verlag, 1919. 2nd ed., 1922. 66 p., 85 ill. First monograph on Lehmbruck, includes statements by the artist (p. 57–62) and oeuvre catalog.

12. *Wilhelm-Lehmbruck-Museum, Duisburg*. Duisburg: Carl Lange Verlag, 1964. 80 p., 33 ill. Issued in conjunction with the opening of the Museum. Includes letters by Ossip Zadkine, Jacques Lipchitz, Ludwig Meidner and Alexander Archipenko; reprints of bibl. 40, 103, 119; and contributions by Gerhard Händler, August Hoff, Manfred Lehmbruck, Siegfried Salzmann, Gustav Stein and Paul Westheim.

articles on lehmbruck

13. AU-BECK, Gustav. "Wilhelm Lehmbruck, zur Gesamtausstellung seiner Werke bei Levesque (Paris)." *Die Plastik* (Munich) 4 (1914): 58–60.

14. B., J. "Münchner Frühlingsausstellung." *Frankfurter Zeitung* (Frankfurt a. M.), (4 Mar. 1915).

15. BADT, Kurt. "Die Plastik Wilhelm Lehmbrucks." *Zeitschrift für bildende Kunst* (Leipzig) Neue Folge 31 (1920): 169–182.

16. BALZER, Werner. "Lehmbruck." *Freie Presse* (Leipzig), (4 Jan. 1921).

17. BARABAN, P. "Lehmbruck aus Meiderich." *Ruhrgebiet: Landschaft-Kultur-Wissenschaft* (Essen) 14, no. 1 (1961): 71–74.

18. BARTHEL, Gustav. "Wilhelm Lehmbruck zum Gedächtnis." *Die Weltkunst* (Munich) 20, no. 3 (1950): 7–8.

19. BEENKEN, Hermann. "Kunstausstellung Bleekers und Lehmbruck." *Bremer Nachrichten* (Bremen), (26 July 1916).

20. BEHRENDT, Walter G. "Zur Kollektiv-Ausstellung in der Galerie Levesque, Paris." *Kunst und Künstler* (Berlin) 12 (1913/14): 649–650.

21. BENNINGHOFF, Ludwig. "Neue Hexenprozesse: Lehmbrucks Kniende." *Der Kreis* (Hamburg) 5 (1927): 473–478.

22. BENSON, Ernest M. "Seven Sculptors." *American Magazine of Art* (New York) 28 (Aug 1935): 461–464.

23. "Berner Kunstausstellung, Kunsthalle." *Neue Zürcher Zeitung* (Zürich) no. 1333 (3 Sept. 1919), 2nd evening ed.

24. BETHGE, Hans. "An Wilhelm Lehmbruck, Gedicht; Worte am Grab." *Aussaat* (Lorch-Stuttgart) 2/3, no. 6/7 (1947/48): 212–213.

25. BETHGE, Hans. "Auf einen Mädchenkopf, Gedicht." *Das Kunstblatt* (Weimar) 2 (1918): 118.

25a. Reprinted in *Aussaat* (Lorch-Stuttgart) 2/3, no. 1/2 (1947/48): 190. See also bibl. 1.

26. BETHGE, Hans. "Der Bildhauer Wilhelm Lehmbruck." *Hellweg* (Essen) 1 (1922/24): 5–6.

27. BETHGE, Hans. "Wilhelm Lehmbruck,†." *Kunst und Künstler* (Berlin) 17 (1918/19): 329–332.

28. BETHGE, Hans. "Wilhelm Lehmbruck zum Gedächtnis." *Museum der Gegenwart* (Berlin) 1, no. 4 (1931): 155–156.

29. BETHGE, Hans. "Lehmbruck." *Das Kunstblatt* (Weimar) 5 (1921): 253–254.

30. BEYER, Oskar. "Wilhelm Lehmbruck." *Die neue Schau* (Cassel) 15 (1954): 117–119.

31. BEYER, Oskar. "Wilhelm Lehmbruck." *Velhagen und Klasings Monatshefte* (Leipzig) 35 (1920): 312–320.

32. BREUER, R. "Der Bildhauer Wilhelm Lehmbruck." *Deutsche Republik* (Frankfurt a. M.) 5, (1927), p. 586 ff.

33. BREUNING, Margaret. "Art in New York." *Parnassus* (New York) 9 (Nov. 1937): 37.

34. BREUNING, Margaret. "Lehmbruck." *Magazine of Art* (New York) 32 (Apr. 1939): 232–234.

35. C. "Lehmbruck." *Der Cicerone* (Leipzig) 11 (1919): 191–192.

36. "Chronik: Rheinische Kunstpflege." *Kunst und Künstler* (Berlin) 26 (1927/28): 39.

37. "Contemporary German Sculpture Acquired: Standing Woman." *St. Louis Museum Bulletin* (St. Louis) 35, no. 3 (1950), 35: 46.

38. COOLIDGE, John. "Wilhelm Lehmbruck's Walking Girl." *Art Bulletin* (New York) 40 (1958): 71–73.

39. CREMERS, Paul J. "Lehmbruck-Ausstellung in Duisburg." *Hellweg* (Essen) 5 (1925): 515–517.

40. DÄUBLER, Theodor. Foreword to *Sonder-Katalog der Kollektiv-Ausstellung Wilhelm Lehmbruck* (Berlin). Kunsthalle Mannheim, 12 Nov., 6 Dec. 1916.

41. D'HAM, Ernest. "Das Lebenswerk Lehmbrucks im Kunstmuseum." *Kulturblätter, Städtische Bühnen Duisburg* (Duisburg) 6, no. 3 (1955/56), 6: 5–8.

42. DIETRICH, Bárbara. "La escultura alemana de principios de siglo: Lehmbruck y Barlach." *Goya* (Madrid) 69 (1965/66): 150–155.

43. DITTGEN, Wilhelm. "Zum Gedenken an Wilhelm Lehmbruck." *Unser Niederrhein* (Dinslaken) 12, no. 2 (1969): 20–21.

44. ECKSTEIN, Hans. "Vergeistigung des Leibes: Wiederbegegnung mit dem Werk Wilhelm Lehmbrucks." *Bildende Kunst* (Berlin) 2, no. 8 (1948): 23–24.

45. EINEM, Herbert von. "Der Weg Wilhelm Lehmbrucks: Rede zum 80. Geburtstag des Künstlers am 4. Januar 1961 im Rathaus zu Duisburg." *Duisburger Forschungen* (Duisburg) 13 (1969): 1–14.

46. EINEM, Herbert von. "Zum Werk Wilhelm Lehmbrucks." *Die Sammlung* (Göttingen) 2 (1946/47): 38–54.

47. ELSEN, Albert. "Lehmbruck." In: *McGraw Hill Dictionary of Art*. Vol. 3, 402. New York, London and Toronto: McGraw Hill Book Co., Inc., 1969.

48. ERLEY, Willy. "Wilhelm Lehmbruck, Spross eines Gehlener Geschlechts." *Heimatkalender für den Kreis Dinslaken* (Dinslaken) 12 (1955): 64–65.

49. "Exhibition of Wilhelm Lehmbruck and his Contemporaries at the Valentin Gallery." *Art Digest* (New York) 26 (15 Oct. 1951): 17.

50. F., K. "Ausstellung: Hagen in Westfalen." *Der Cicerone* (Leipzig) 4 (1912): 318.

51. FECHNER, Peter P. "Lehmbruck." *Stuttgarter Rundschau* (Stuttgart), no. 7 (1948), 3: 21–23.

52. FECHNER, Peter P. "Wilhelm Lehmbruck." *Die Welt der Frau* (Stuttgart) 3 (2 Sept. 1948): 4–5.

53. Feuilleton, Kleine Chronik: "Aus dem Zürcher Kunsthaus." *Neue Zürcher Zeitung* (Zurich) no. 294 (18 Feb. 1917).

54. Feuilleton, Kleine Chronik: "Zürcher Kunstchronik." *Neue Zürcher Zeitung* (Zurich) no. 1483 (6 Nov. 1918).

55. Feuilleton, Kunstchronik: "Aus dem Zürcher Kunsthaus." *Neue Zeitung* (Zurich), 2 Feb. 1916.

56. FRANCK, Hans. "Lehmbruck." *Die Rheinlande* (Düsseldorf) 30 (1920): 65–72.

57. FRANCK, Hans. "Lehmbruck." *Die Gegenwart* (Berlin) 50 (1921): 52.

58. FRANCK, Hans. "Wilhelm Lehmbruck." *Das Tor: Düsseldorfer Heimatblätter* (Düsseldorf) 20 (1954): 42–47.

59. FRANCK, Hans. "Wilhelm Lehmbruck." *Weser Zeitung* (Bremen), 10 Oct. and 11 Oct. 1921.

60. FRANKEL, Robert. "Modigliani and Lehmbruck, Contrasts in Great Artistic Personalities." *Art News* (New York) 36 (6 Nov. 1937): 15.

61. Franz Metzner†—"Wilhelm Lehmbruck†". *Die Kunst für Alle* (Munich) 34 (1918/19): 300. (*Die Kunst* 39 (1918/19): 300).

62. "Gedenktage der Kunst und Wissenschaft: Wilhelm Lehmbruck." *Rhein- und Ruhrzeitung* (Duisburg) no. 150 (Morgenausgabe 4 Apr. 1919), p. 3.

63. GERSTENBERG, Kurt. "Freie Secession Berlin, Sommerausstellung mit Gedächtnisausstellungen für Theo von Brockhausen und Wilhelm Lehmbruck." *Der Cicerone* (Leipzig) 11 (1919): 463.

64. GIEDION-WELCKER, Carola, "Macke, Marc et Lehmbruck à la Kunsthalle de Berne." *Les Arts plastiques* (Brussels) 9/10 (1948): 420–422.

65. GRAUTOFF, Otto. "Zur Kollektiv-Ausstellung in der Galerie Levesque, Paris." *Der Cicerone* (Leipzig) 6 (1914): 539–540.

66. GROHMANN, Will. "Wilhelm Lehmbruck." In: *Thieme-Becker Allgemeines Lexikon der bildenden Kunst*, Vol. 22, 584. Leipzig: Seemann, 1928.

67. GROM, Ludwig. "Münchner Neue Sezession, III. Graphische Ausstellung, Gedächtnisausstellung Wilhelm Lehmbruck." *Feuer* (Weimar) 2 (1920/21): 724.

68. GRUNEWALD, M. "Wilhelm Lehmbruck." *Deutsches Volkstum* (Hamburg) (1921): 142–145.

69. HÄNDLER, Gerhard. "Wilhelm Lehmbruck in den Ausstellungen und der Kritik seiner Zeit." *Duisburger Forschungen* (Duisburg) 13 (1969): 21–82.

70. HÄNDLER, Gerhard. "Wilhelm Lehmbruck, Mädchen sich umwendend." In: *Museum und Kunst, Beiträge für Alfred Hentzen*. Hamburg: Hans Christiansen, [n.d.] 64–82.

71. HÄNDLER, Gerhard. "Wilhelm-Lehmbruck-Museum der Stadt Duisburg." *Wallraf-Richartz Jahrbuch* (Cologne) 32 (1970): 327–33.

72. HARTMANN, A. G. "Wilhelm Lehmbruck Gedächtnisausstellung." *Der Tag* (Berlin), 7 Feb. 1920.

73. HAUSENSTEIN, A. "Zum Tode Wilhelm Lehmbrucks." *Münchner Neueste Nachrichten* (Munich) no. 149 (1919).

74. HEUER, Alfred. "Wilhelm Lehmbruck" (Das war verfemte Kunst, no. 24) *Aussaat* (Lorch-Stuttgart) 2/3, no. 6/7 (1947/48): 208–211.

75. "Hidden Gothic: Kneeling Woman by Lehmbruck acquired by Chicago." *Art Digest* (New York) 14 (15 May 1940): 12.

76. HILDEBRANDT, Hans. "Wilhelm Lehmbruck." *Funk-Illustrierte* (Stuttgart) 17, no. 36 (2 Oct. 1949).

77. HOFF, August. "Wilhelm Lehmbrucks Werk." *Kölner Woche* (Cologne) no. 16 (1925).

78. HOFF, August. "Zu Wilhelm Lehmbrucks Gedächtnis." *Kunst und Kirche* (Berlin) 6 (1929/30): 131.

79. HOPE, Henry R. "Lehmbruck." In: *Encyclopedia of World Art*, Vol. 9, 198–9 New York, London and Toronto: McGraw-Hill Book Co., Inc., 1964.

80. J., M. "Wilhelm Lehmbruck Gedächtnisausstellung bei Paul Cassirer." *Deutsche Allgemeine Zeitung* (Berlin), 7 Feb. 1920.

81. JAEHNER, Horst. "Lehmbruck und die 'heimliche Gotik'." *Bildende Kunst* (Munich) 4, no. 6 (1956): 322–324.

82. JOLLOS, Werner. "Das Erbe Wilhelm Lehmbrucks." *Das Kunstblatt* (Berlin) 15 (1931): 260.

83. JUNGHANS, Fritz. "Ein Klassiker der Moderne: Wilhelm Lehmbruck." *Die Kommenden* (Freiburg im Br.) 11, no. 20 (1957): 5.

84. KAESTNER, Erich. "Wilhelm Lehmbruck." *Die Weltbühne* (Berlin) no. 33 (16 Sept. 1927), 270.

85. KIRCHNER, Joachim. "Westheims Lehmbruck'." *Der Cicerone* (Leipzig) 12 (1920): 265.

86. "Kleine Mitteilungen." *Münchner Neueste Nachrichten* (Munich), 30 June 1914 and 24 May 1916.

87. KUHN, Alfred. "Lehmbruck, Wilhelm." Bildhauer. *Deutsches Biographisches Jahrbuch* (Stuttgart), 1914–1920.

88. KUNTZ, E. "Spitzenpreise für Lehmbruck." *Der Kunsthandel* (Heidelberg) 3, no. 5 (1961): 21–22.

89. KURTH, Willy. "Wilhelm Lehmbruck." *Kunst für Alle* (Berlin) 35 (1919/20): 145–154.

90. L., Dr. D. "Franz Metzner und Wilhelm Lehmbruck." *Der Kunstwanderer* (Berlin) 11 (1929): 369.

91. LEHMBRUCK, Manfred. "Erinnerungen an meinen Vater." *Kunst der Nation* (Berlin) 2 (15 Nov. 1933).

92. LEHMBRUCK, Willi. "Wilhelm Lehmbruck. Das Werk und seine Quellen." In: *Minuscula discipulorum, Kunsthistorische Studien Hans Kauffmann zum 70. Geburtstag, 1966.* Ed. Tillmann, Buddensieg und Winner, Berlin: Bruno Hessling, (1968): 177–185.

92a. LEHMBRUCK, Willi. "Wilhelm Lehmbruck und die Antike: Anregungen und Eindrücke aus dem Bereich der mediterranen Kunst." In: *Duisburger Forschungen* (Duisburg) 13 (1969): 83–92. Reprint of bibl. 92.

93. "Die Lehmbruck Ausstellung im Behnhaus." *Lübeckische Blätter, Zeitschrift der Gesellschaft zur Förderung gemeinnütziger Tätigkeit* (Lübeck) 92, no. 12 (1956) 162–163.

94. "Lehmbruck and other German Sculptors at Gerson Gallery." *Art News* (New York) 61 (Feb. 1963): 17.

95. [Lehmbruck Exhibition, Museum of Modern Art]. *Art News* (New York) 28 (15 Mar. 1930): 11.

96. [Lehmbruck Exhibition, Buchholz Gallery]. *Art News* (New York) 40 (1 Dec. 1941): 32.

97. [Lehmbruck Exhibition, Marie Harriman's]. *Art News* (New York) 37 (25 Feb. 1939): 15.

98. "Lehmbrucks Frühwerk in Duisburg." *Das Kunstblatt* (Berlin) 10 (1926): 391.

99. "Lehmbruck and Maillol at Buchholz Gallery." *Art Digest* (New York) 16 (1 Dec. 1941): 6.

100. LUUZ, W. A. "Zum 10 jährigen Todestag von Wilhelm Lehmbruck." *Rheinischer Beobachter* (Cologne) 5 (1929): 76.

101. MAACK, Charlotte. "Abschiednehmende Worte zur Tübinger Wilhelm-Lehmbruck-Ausstellung." *Das Goldene Tor* (Lahr) 3, no. 8 (1948): 813–815.

102. MASSARD, Jules. "Wilhelm Lehmbruck." *Emporium* (Bergamo) 124 (1956): 164–168.

103. MEIER-GRAEFE, Julius. Paris 1910/11. *Frankfurter Zeitung* (Frankfurt), Reichsausgabe, no. 9–11 (5 Jan. 1932): 9. Reprinted in bibl. 10, 12 and Exhibition Catalog, Mannheim, 1949.

104. MEIER-GRAEFE, Julius. "Pariser Reaktionen." *Kunst und Künstler* (Berlin) 10 (1911/12): 444–448.

105. METTKE, Heidrun. "Die Bildwerke von Wilhelm Lehmbruck in der Dresdener Skulpturensammlung." *Dresdener Kunstblätter* (Dresden) 10, no. 1 (1966): 4–8.

106. MÜLLER, Karl. "Wilhelm Lehmbrucks Weg und Werk." *Die Westmark, Monatszeitschrift für deutsche Kultur* (Neustadt a. d. Weinstrasse) 2 (1934/35): 304–307.

107. "New York Views Lehmbruck's Expressionism." *Art Digest* (New York) 13 (1 Mar. 1939): 15.

108. ODENHEIMER, Dennis. "Lehmbruck's Bust of the Kneeling Woman Acquired by Chicago." *Chicago Art Institute Bulletin* (Chicago) 34 (Mar. 1940): 41–42.

109. OSBORN, Max. "Lehmbruck Gedächtnisausstellung bei Paul Cassirer. *Vossische Zeitung* (Berlin), 3 Feb. 1920.

110. PANKOK-DROSTE, H. "Bekenntnisse zu Wilhelm Lehmbruck." *Der Scheinwerfer* (Essen) 1, no. 9 (1927/28), no. 11: 14.

111. PANNENBECKER, Emmi. "Lehmbruck Heiter?" *Duisburger Forschungen* (Duisburg) 13 (1969): 117–123.

112. PASSARGE, Walter. "Wilhelm Lehmbruck." In: *Die grossen Deutschen*. Vol. 5, Berlin, Propyläen-Verlag (1957): 469–478.

113. PEAT, W. D. "Lehmbruck's Bust of a Young Woman." *John Herron Institute Bulletin* (Indianapolis) 22 (Oct. 1945): 30–31.

114. PFEIL, K. G. "Wilhelm Lehmbruck zum 50. Geburtstag." *Germania* (Berlin), (4 Jan. 1931).

115. RAYNOR, Vincent. "Lehmbruck and Contemporaries at Gerson." *Arts Magazine* (New York) 37 (Apr. 1963): 52.

116. RICH, Daniel Catton. "Standing Woman, Composition Stone by Wilhelm Lehmbruck." *Chicago Art Institute Bulletin* (Chicago) 28 (Sept. 1934): 66.

116a. Also in: *Art Digest* (New York) 9 (15 Oct. 1934): 32.

RODEN, Günter von, and Siegfried SALZMANN, eds. *Wilhelm Lehmbruck, Sieben Beiträge zum Gedenken seines 50. Todestages*. Duisburg, Walter Braun Verlag, 1969. (*Duisburger Forschungen*, Vol. 13). See bibl. 45, 69, 92a, 111, 120, 130, 141a.

117. "Rundschau: Sammlungen: Duisburg." *Der Cicerone* (Leipzig) 18 (1926): 67.

118. "Rundschau: Sammlungen: Duisburg." *Der Cicerone*, (Leipzig) 18 (1926): 717.

119. SALMON, André. Préface. In catalog: "Exposition des oeuvres de Wilhelm Lehmbruck," Galérie Levesque & Cie, 109 Faubourg Saint-Honoré, Paris. 20–30 June 1914. Reprinted in bibl. 12.

120. SALZMANN, Siegfried. "Wie die 'Duisburgerin' nach Duisburg kam." *Duisburger Forschungen* (Duisburg) 13 (1969): 93–100.

121. SCHACHT, Richard. "Wilhelm Lehmbruck." *Freie Deutsche Bühne*, (Berlin) 2 (1920): 662–665.

122. SCHÄFER, Wilhelm. "Wilhelm Lehmbruck." *Die Reinlande* (Düsseldorf) 15 (1915): 293–300.

123. SCHÄFERDIEK, Willi. "Der Bildhauer Wilhelm Lehmbruck. Zur zehnten Wiederkehr seines Todestages." *Die Werrag* no. 12 (24 Mar. 1929).

124. S[CHEFFLER], K[arl]. "Berliner Ausstellungen: Lehmbruck-Ausstellung." *Der Cicerone* (Leipzig) 12 (1920): 127–128.

125. SCHEFFLER, Karl. "Galérie Levesque, Paris. Exposition Lehmbruck." *Kunst und Künstler* (Berlin) 12 (1913/14).

126. SCHEFFLER, Karl. "Gedächtnisausstellung Wilhelm Lehmbruck bei Paul Cassirer 1920." *Kunst und Künstler* (Berlin) 18 (1919/20): 341.

127. SCHLÖSSER, Manfred. "Wilhelm Lehmbruck." *Baukunst und Werkform* (Heidelberg) 9, no. 12 (1956): 690.

128. SCHMIDT, Paul F. "Aus dem Berliner Kunstleben. Lehmbruck - Berliner Humor- Junge Künstler." *Königsberger Allgemeine Zeitung* (Königsberg), (27 Mar. 1929).

129. SCHUBERT, Dietrich. "Frühwerke Wilhelm Lehmbrucks: Zur Sonder-Ausstellung seiner zwischen 1896 und 1910 entstandenen Arbeiten im Wilhelm-Lehmbruck-Museum Duisburg." *Kunstchronik* (Munich) 23 (1970): 147–151.

130. SCHUBERT, Dietrich. "Lehmbrucks *Pietà*. Ein Beispiel einer Gestaltverwandlung." *Duisburger Forschungen* (Duisburg) 13 (1969): 101–116.

131. SCHWARZ, K. "Wilhelm Lehmbruck." *Deutsche Kunst und Dekoration* (Darmstadt) 45 (1919/20): 43–49.

132. "The Sculpture of Wilhelm Lehmbruck. An Exhibition at the Tate Gallery." *Illustrated London News* (London) 1 (1957): 1031.

133. "Stadt Duisburg ehrt einen Bergmann-Sohn. Das neue Wilhelm Lehmbruck Museum." *Gewerkschaftliche Rundschau für die Bergbau- und Energiewirtschaft* (Bochum) 18, no. 2 (1965): 108–110.

134. STILLER, Richard. "Lehmbruck bei Arnold." *Dresdner Anzeiger* (Dresden), (17 Mar. 1921).

135. TRIER, Eduard. "Die Lehmbruck-Stiftung des Kulturkreises." *Jahresring* (Stuttgart) 6 (1959/60): 384–588.

136. TRIER, Eduard. "Wilhelm Lehmbruck." *Der Ausschnitt* (Bochum) 11, no. 6 (Dec. 1959): 28–33.

137. TRIER, Eduard. "Wilhelm Lehmbruck. Paris 1910/14." *Jahresring* (Stuttgart) 2 (1955/56): 144–153.

138. TRIER, Eduard. "Wilhelm Lehmbruck und die Kunst des 20. Jahrhunderts." *Universitas* (Stuttgart) 15 (1960): 1191–1202.

139. "Tuaillon und Lehmbruck." *Ganymed* (Dresden) 1 (1919): 91.

140. TURKEL-DERI, Frida. "Berlin Letter." *Art News* (New York) 30 (9 Jan. 1932).

141. UNRUH, Fritz von. "Wilhelm Lehmbruck." *College Art Journal* (New York) 16, no. 4 (Winter 1956/57): 274–279.

141a. UNRUH, Fritz von. "Begegnung mit Wilhelm Lehmbruck." *Duisburger Forschungen* (Duisburg) 13 (1969): 15–20. German translation of bibl. 141.

142. WATSON, F. "Lehmbruck Exhibition, Museum of Modern Art." *Arts* (New York) 16 (20 Apr. 1930): 567–568.

143. WEISS, Karl. "Gedächtnisausstellung der Neuen Sezession: Wilhelm Lehmbruck." *Münchner Neueste Nachrichten* (Munich), July 1921).

144. WEISS, Karl. "Wilhelm Lehmbruck." *Die Plastik* (Munich) 11 (1921): 41–42.

145. WERNER, Alfred. "The Tender Monumentality of Wilhelm Lehmbruck." *American Artist* (Stamford, Conn.) 29, no. 6 (June 1965): 54–59, 88–91.

146. WESTHEIM, Paul. "Glossen: Meister Lehmbruck." *Wieland* (Munich & Berlin) 5, no. 11 (1919/20): 1–5.

147. WESTHEIM, Paul. "Heimaturlaub zur Kunst. Zur Ausstellung der 'Freien Sezession' in Berlin." *Frankfurter Zeitung* (Frankfurt) no. 61, 1. Morgenblatt, (2 Mar. 1916).

148. WESTHEIM, Paul. "Lehmbruck." *Cahiers de Belgique* (Brussels) (1929): 195–201.

149. WESTHEIM, Paul. "Lehmbrucks Lehr- und Werdejahre." *Feuer* (Weimar) 1 (1920): 7–15.

150. WESTHEIM, Paul. "Recuerdos de Wilhelm Lehmbruck." *Novedades, Mexico en la cultura* (Mexico City) no. 41 (13 Nov. 1949).

151. WESTHEIM, Paul. "Umschau: Mutter und Kind von Lehmbruck." *Das Kunstblatt* (Berlin) 6 (1922): 221–222.

152. WESTHEIM, Paul. "Unbekanntes Frühwerk von Wilhelm Lehmbruck." *Das Kunstblatt* (Berlin) 12 (1928): 305.

153. WESTHEIM, Paul. [Wilhelm Lehmbruck.] *Frankfurter Zeitung* (Frankfurt a.M.), (4 Apr. 1919).

154. WESTHEIM, Paul. "Wilhelm Lehmbruck." *Das Kunstblatt* (Berlin) 3 (1919): 193–200.

155. WHITTEL, George S. "London Commentary." *The Studio* (London) 154 (Sept. 1954): 91–92.

156. [Wilhelm Lehmbruck.] *Der Tag*: Illustrierte Unterhaltung (Berlin) no. 3 (4 Jan. 1913).

157. "Wilhelm Lehmbruck." *Tägliche Rundschau* (Berlin), (11 June 1915).

158. "Wilhelm Lehmbruck." *Antiquitäten-Rundschau* (Eisenach) 23 (1925): 225.

159. "Wilhelm Lehmbruck." *General-Anzeiger* (Duisburg), (12 June 1915).

160. "Wilhelm Lehmbruck." *Hamburger Nachrichten* (Hamburg), (7 Feb. 1921).

161. "Wilhelm Lehmbruck." *Neue Zürcher Zeitung* (Zurich), (8 June 1919).

162. "Wilhelm Lehmbruck." *Räder, Zeitschrift für die Arbeit am Wiederaufbau* (Berlin) 10 (1929): 148.

163. "Wilhelm Lehmbruck." *Vossische Zeitung* (Berlin), (11 June 1915).

164. WOLFRADT, Willi. "Wilhelm Lehm-bruck†." *Das Junge Deutschland* (Berlin) 2 (1919): 238–240.

165. ZAHN, A. "Wilhelm Lehmbruck." *Tausendjahrfeier Duisburg-Beeck* (Duisburg), (1925): 34–37.

general studies

166. APOLLINAIRE, Guillaume. *Chroniques d'Art*. Paris: Gallimard, 1960, p. 161, 165, 229, 401–402. Reprint of review of Galérie Levesque exhibition from *Paris Journal* (28 June 1914).

167. ARNASON, H. Harvard. *History of Modern Art: Painting, Sculpture, Architecture*. New York: Abrams, 1968. p. 132–134.

168. AUST, Günter. "Die Ausstellung des Sonderbundes 1912 in Köln." *Wallraf-Richartz Jahrbuch* (Cologne) 23 (1962): 275–292.

169. "Die Ausstellung der Freien Sezession." *Vossische Zeitung* (Berlin), (5 Jan. 1915).

170. BAZIN, Germain. *The History of World Sculpture*. Greenwich, Conn.: New York Graphic Society, 1968.

171. BENDEMANN, Eduard von. "Deutsche Kunst, Darmstadt 1918." *Deutsche Kunst und Dekoration* (Darmstadt) 42 (1918): 159.

172. BENDER, Ewald. "XXIV Ausstellung der Berliner Secession 1912." *Deutsche Kunst und Dekoration* (Darmstadt) 15 (1911/12): 294.

173. BENDER, Paul. "Drahtplastik." *Das Kunstwerk* (Baden-Baden) 10, no. 1–2 (1956/57), 10: 9–12.

174. BENSON, Ernest M. "Modern German Sculpture, A Discussion of Contemporary Trends." *Parnassus* (New York) 5 (Apr. 1933): 7–11.

175. BEYER, Oskar. *Religiöse Plastik unserer Zeit*. Berlin: Furche Verlag, 1924. p. 17–18.

176. BIERMANN, Georg. "Enquète sur la sculpture moderne en Allemagne et en France." *Cahiers d'Art* (Paris), 1928, p. 383–385.

177. BIERMANN, Georg. "XXIV. Ausstellung der Berliner Secession 1912." *Der Cicerone* (Leipzig) 4 (1912): 309–311.

178. BROWN, Milton. *The Story of the Armory Show*. New York: Joseph H. Hirschhorn Foundation, 1963. p. 47, 108, 119, 171.

179. BUTTLAR, Herbert von. "Antike Plastik und Plastik der Gegenwart." *Marburger Jahrbuch für Kunstwissenschaft* (Marburg) 15 (1949/50): 251–272.

180. CANADAY, John. *Mainstreams of Modern Art*. New York: Simon and Schuster, 1959. p. 441–442.

181. CHANIN, A. L. "The Henry Pearlman Collection." *Connoisseur* (London) 145 (1960): 230–236.

182. COLOMBIER, Pierre du. *L'Art allemand*. Paris, 1946. p. 135.

183. DÄUBLER, Theodor. *Der Neue Standpunkt*. Leipzig: Insel-Verlag, 1919. p. 187–88.

183a. Reprint: Dresden: Jess, 1957, p. 162–163.

184. EINSTEIN, Carl. *Die Kunst des 20. Jahrhunderts*. Berlin: Propyläen, 1926 (Propyläen-Kunstgeschichte Vol. 16). p. 166–168.

185. ELIAS, Julius. "Salon d'Automne, Paris 8ᵉ Exposition. Grand Palais des Champs Elysées." *Kunst und Künstler* (Berlin) 9 (1910/11): p. 308 f.

186. ELSEN, Albert. *Purposes of Art*. New York: Holt, Rinehart & Winston, Inc., 1962. 2nd ed., 1967.

187. FAULKNER, Ray & Edwin Ziegfeld. *Art Today*. New York: Holt, Rinehart & Winston, Inc., 1969. p. 454.

188. FISCHER, William Murrell. "Sculpture at the Exhibition." *Arts and Decoration* (New York) 3 (1912/13): 168 f.

189. FORTLAGE, Arnold. "Deutsche Kunstausstellung Köln, 1906, in der 'Flora' Ausstellung des Verbandes der Kunstfreunde in den Ländern am Rhein." *Die Rheinlande* (Düsseldorf) 7 (1906): 44.

190. FORTLAGE, Arnold. "Die Internationale Kunstausstellung des Sonderbundes in Köln." *Der Cicerone* (Leipzig) 4 (1912): 554 f.

191. FORTLAGE, Arnold. "Die Internationale Kunstausstellung des Sonderbundes in Köln." *Kunst für Alle* (Berlin) 28 (1912/13): 84–93.

192. FR., J. "Münchner Neue Sezession." *Berliner Tageblatt* (Berlin), 9 June 1915.

193. FRIEDEBERGER, Hans. "Freie Secession Berlin, 1. Ausstellung." *Der Cicerone* (Leipzig) 6 (1914): 270.

194. FRIEDEBERGER, Hans. "Freie Secession Berlin, 2. Ausstellung 1916." *Der Cicerone* (Leipzig) 8 (1916): 192 f.

195. FRIEDEBERGER, Hans. "XXV. Ausstellung der Berliner Secession, Zeichnende Künste." *Der Cicerone* (Leipzig) 4 (1912): 896.

196. GEORGI, Walter. "Freie Secession Berlin, 1. Ausstellung 1914." *Deutsche Kunst und Dekoration* (Darmstadt) 34 (1914): 157–166.

197. GERSTENBERG, Kurt. "Wilhelm Lehmbrucks Radierungen." *Das Graphische Jahrbuch* (Darmstadt), n.d. [ca. 1919]: 37–38.

198. GERTZ, Ulrich. *Plastik der Gegenwart.* Berlin: Rembrandt-Verlag, 1953, Vol. I, p. 50–52. (Die Kunst unserer Zeit, Vol. 8).

199. GIEDION-WELCKER, Carola. *Moderne Plastik: Elemente der Wirklichkeit, Masse und Auflockerung.* Zurich: H. Girsberger, 1937.

199a. English translation. *Modern Plastic Art.* Zurich: H. Girsberger, 1937.

200. GIEDION-WELCKER, Carola. *Die Plastik des 20. Jahrhunderts: Volumen und Raumgestaltung.* Stuttgart: Gerd Hatje, 1955. Revised ed. of bibl. 199.

200a. English translation: *Contemporary Sculpture, an Evolution in Volume and Form.* New York: Wittenborn, 1955; 2nd ed. 1960, p. 14, 34–37, 84, 106, 336, 338.

201. GLASER, Curt. "Die Geschichte der Berliner Secession." *Kunst und Künstler* (Berlin) 26 (1927/28): 14–20, 66–70.

202. GLASER, Curt. *Die Graphik der Neuzeit.* Berlin: Bruno Cassirer, 1922, p. 553–554.

203. GLASER, Curt. "Die XXIV. Ausstellung der Berliner Secession." *Kunst für Alle* (Berlin) 27 (1911/12): 413–431.

204. GLASER, Curt. "Die XXVI. Ausstellung der Berliner Secession." *Kunst für Alle* (Berlin) 28 (1912/13): 457–474.

205. GLASER, Curt. "Die Winterausstellung der Berliner Secession." *Kunst für Alle* (Berlin) 28 (1912/13): 179–180.

206. GRAUTOFF, Otto. "30. Ausstellung der 'Indépendents.'" *Der Cicerone* (Leipzig) 6 1914): 217.

207. G[RAUTOFF], O[tto]. "Kunstausstellungen: Paris." *Kunst und Künstler* (Berlin) 12 (1913/14): 649.

208. GRAUTOFF, Otto. "Salon d'Automne, Paris Grand Palais." *Der Cicerone* (Leipzig), (1913): 844 f.

209. GROHMANN, Will. *L'art contemporain en Allemagne.* Cahiers d'Art (Paris), (1938): 1–12.

210. GROHMANN, Will. *Bildende Kunst und Architektur zwischen den Kriegen.* Berlin: Suhrkamp, 1953, p. 245, 249, 252–255, 447.

211. GROHMANN, Will. "Deutsche Plastik des 20. Jahrhunderts: Barlach, Lehmbruck, Marcks." *Universitas* (Stuttgart) 9 (1954): 243–250.

212. GROHMANN, Will. "Enquète sur la sculpture moderne en Allemagne et en France." *Cahiers d'Art* (Paris), (1928) p. 371–372.

213. GROHMANN, Will. *Scultura tedesca del secolo XX.* Dedalo (Milan), 1933, p. 34–62.

214. GROTE, Ludwig. *Deutsche Kunst im 20. Jahrhundert.* Munich: Prestel, 1953.

215. GRZIMEK, Waldemar. *Deutsche Bildhauer des 20. Jahrhunderts.* Munich: Heinz Moos, 1969, p. 118–120, 273–279.

216. HAFTMANN, Werner. "Neuerwerbungen der Nationalgalerie 1968." *Jahrbuch Preussischer Kulturbesitz* (Berlin), 1968, p. 197–204.

217. HAMANN, Richard. *Geschichte der Kunst.* Berlin: Knaur, 1933, p. 875.

218. HAMILTON, George Heard. *Painting and Sculpture in Europe: 1880–1940.* Baltimore, Md.: Penguin Books, 1967. (Pelican History of Art).

219. HAMMACHER, A. M. *The Evolution of Modern Sculpture: Tradition and Innovation.* New York: Abrams, 1968, p. 107, 146–148, 151.

220. HARTLAUB, G. F. *Die Graphik des Expressionismus.* Stuttgart: Gerd Hatje, 1947, p. 46.

221. HAUSENSTEIN, Wilhelm. *Die bildende Kunst der Gegenwart: Malerei, Plastik, Zeichnungen.* Berlin & Stuttgart: Deutsche Verlagsanstalt, 1914. 2nd ed., 1919; 3nd ed., 1923.

222. HEISE, Carl Georg. "Neuerwerbungen moderner Plastik." *Jahrbuch der Hamburger Kunstsammlungen* (Hamburg) 1 (1948): 4–7.

223. HENTZEN, Alfred. *Deutsche Bildhauer der Gegenwart.* Berlin: Rembrandt-Verlag, 1935, p. 28 f.

224. HENTZEN, Alfred. "La Sculpture." In: *L'Art allemand contemporain.* Offenburg, 1951.

225. HENTZEN, Alfred. "La Sculpture." *Documents 1951,* (Paris) numéro spécial, p. 50–59.

226. HESS, Walter. "Cronica de Munich." *Goya* (Madrid) no. 10 (1956): 270–273.

227. HILDEBRANDT, Hans. *Die Kunst des 19. und 20. Jahrhunderts.* Wildpark-Potsdam: Akademische Verlagsgesellschaft Athenaion, 1924, p. 487. (Handbuch der Kunstwissenschaft).

228. HILDEBRANDT, Hans. "Die zweite Sommerausstellung der Münchner 'Neuen Secession.'" *Deutsche Kunst und Dekoration* (Darmstadt) 38 (1916): 295–307.

229. HOFMANN, Werner. *Die Plastik des 20. Jahrhunderts.* Frankfurt: Fischer, 1958, p. 69–72.

230. HUGGLER, Max. "Die Neuerwerbungen des Berner Kunstmuseums." *Das Werk* (Winterthur) (1952): 303–308.

231. HUNTER, Sam. *Modern American Painting and Sculpture.* New York: Dell, 1959, p. 66.

232. J., M. "Sommerausstellung der Neuen Münchner Sezession." *Abendzeitung München und Augsburg* (Munich), (8 June 1918).

233. J., M. "Berner Kunstausstellungen, Kunsthalle." *Neue Zürcher Zeitung* (Zurich) 2. Abendblatt, no. 1333, (3 Sept. 1919).

234. KOLBE, George. *Auf Wegen der Kunst: Schriften, Skizzen, Plastiken.* Berlin-Zehlendorf: Verlag Konrad Lemmer, 1949.

235. KUHN, Alfred. *Die neuere Plastik von 1800 bis zur Gegenwart.* Munich: Delphin-Verlag, 1921, p. 114 f.

236. KUHN, Walt. *The Story of the Armory Show.* New York: Walt Kuhn 1938, p. 14.

237. KURTH, Willy. "Freie Secession Berlin, 4. Ausstellung 1918." *Deutsche Kunst und Dekoration* (Darmstadt) 43 (1918/19): 8.

238. LEIPPIEN, H. R. "Aspekte der neuen Sonderbundausstellung im Wallraf-Richartz Museum." *Museen in Köln Bulletin* (Cologne) no. 16 (1962): 121.

239. LEVINSON, André. "A. T. Matveiév." *Apollon* (Petrograd) no. 8 (1913), p. 5–15.

240. LEY, Walter. "Ausstellungen: Berlin." *Das Kunstblatt* (Berlin) 4, no. 2 (1920), 4:62.

241. LICHT, Fred. *Sculpture, 19th and 20th Century.* Greenwich, Conn.: New York Graphic Society, 1967, p. 330.

242. MAILLARD, Robert, ed. *A Dictionary of Modern Sculpture.* London: Methuen, 1964. New York: Tudor, 1964.

243. MASHECK, Joseph. "Teddy's Taste: Theodore Roosevelt and the Armory Show." *Artforum* (New York) 9, no. 3 (Nov. 1970), 70–73.

244. MATHIESEN, Egon. "Tysk Kunst, Udstillingen i den 'Frie' af nyere tysk kunst." *Tilskueren* (Copenhagen) 1 (1932): 480–492.

245. MAYER, Alfred. "Die Münchner Neue Sezession." *Vossische Zeitung* (Berlin) no. 142 (18 Mar. 1915).

246. MEIER-GRAEFE, Julius. *Entwicklungsgeschichte der modernen Kunst.* Stuttgart: Julius Hoffmann, 1915. 2nd ed. Vol. 3: 551–552; Revised eds. 1927 and 1966.

247. MEYERS, Bernard. *Art and Civilization.* New York and London: McGraw-Hill, 1967.

248. "O nú e o Strip-Tease." *Habitat* (São Paulo) no. 67 (Mar. 1962): 36.

249. OSBORN, Max. "Kunstausstellungen." *Vossische Zeitung* (Berlin), (22 Apr. 1915).

250. OSTEN, Gert von der. *Plastik des 20. Jahrhunderts in Deutschland, Oesterreich und der Schweiz.* Königstein im Taunus: Karl Robert Langewiesche Nachfolger Hans Köster, 1962, p. 4–5. (Die Blauen Bücher).

251. PLATTE, Hans. Plastik. Munich: (Die Kunst des 20. Jahrhunderts, C. G. Heise, ed., 1957, Vol. 2.)

252. PUETZFELD, Carl. "Neue Münchner Sezession." *Dresdner Neueste Nachrichten* (Dresden), (27 June 1915).

253. PUETZFELD, Carl. [Exhibition Review.] *Dresdner Neueste Nachrichten* (Dresden), (4 June 1915).

254. RAMSDEN, E. H. *Sculpture, Theme and Variation.* London: Lund Humphries, 1953.

255. RAVE, Paul Ortwin. *Deutsche Bildnerkunst von Schadow bis zur Gegenwart.* Berlin: Bard, 1929. (Ein Führer zu den Bildwerken der National-Galerie).

256. RAVE, Paul Ortwin. "Dittatura sull' arte nel III Reich." *Sele Arte* (Florence) 18 (1955): 28–39.

257. RAVE, Paul Ortwin. *Kunstdiktatur im Dritten Reich.* Berlin: Gebrüder Mann, 1949, p. 9, 34, 41, 46, 57, 66–67, 69, 70, 73.

258. READ, Herbert. *A Concise History of Modern Sculpture.* New York: Praeger, 1959; 2nd ed. 1962.

259. RITCHIE, Andrew Carnduff. *Sculpture of the Twentieth Century.* New York: Museum of Modern Art, 1952. p. 19–20.

260. ROH, Franz. *Geschichte der deutschen Kunst von 1900 bis zur Gegenwart.* Munich: Bruckmann, 1958. p. 317–318.

260a. ROH, Franz. *German Art in the Twentieth Century.* Greenwich, Conn.: New York Graphic Society, 1968. English translation of bibl. 260.

261. ROHE, M. K. "Die neue Münchner Secession." *Kunst für Alle* (Berlin) 29 (1913/14): 517–526.

262. ROOSEVELT, Theodore. *History as Literature and other Essays.* New York, 1913. Includes reprint of "A Layman's View of an Art Exhibition," discussing the Armory Show, originally published in *The Outlook* (New York), (9 Mar. 1913).

263. ROSE, Barbara. *American Art Since 1900, A Critical History.* New York: Praeger, 1967.

264. ROSENBERG, Jakob. "German Expressionist Printmakers." *Magazine of Art* (Washington) 38 (1945): 300–305.

265. RUPE, Hans. "Ausstellung, München." *Kunstchronik* (Leipzig) N.F. 56 (1920/21): 827–829.

266. SALOMY, Alfred. "Grosse Kunstausstellung Duesseldorf 1920." *Das Kunstblatt* (Berlin) 4 (1920): 241–246.

267. SAUERLAND, Max. *Deutsche Bildhauer um 1900.* Leipzig, Langewiesche, 1925. (Die Blauen Bücher) p. 5, 10.

268. SCHAEFER, Wilhelm. "Zur Sonderbundausstellung in Köln, II: Die Gemessenen." *Frankfurter Zeitung* (Frankfurt a.M.) no. 165. (16 June 1913).

269. SCHEFFLER, Karl. "Berliner Secession." *Kunst und Künstler* (Berlin) 10 (1911/12): 432–441.

270. SCHEFFLER, Karl. "Freie Secession Berlin, 2. Ausstellung 1916." *Kunst und Künstler* (Berlin) 14 (1915/16): 454.

271. SCHEFFLER, Karl. *Geschichte der europäischen Kunst im 19. Jahrhundert.* Berlin: Cassirer, Vol. 2: (1927) 332–334.

272. SCHMIDT, Diether, ed. *Schriften deutscher Künstler des zwanzigsten Jahrhunderts.* Dresden, VEB Verlag der Kunst, 1965. Vol. 1, Manifeste, Manifeste, 1905–1933. p. 128–130.

273. SCHMIDT, Paul Ferdinand. "Galerie Flechtheim, Duesseldorf, Beiträge zur Kunst des 19. Jahrhunderts und unserer Zeit." *Der Cicerone* (Leipzig) 6 (1914): 237 f.

274. SCHMIDT, Robert. "Grosse Berliner Kunstausstellung 1909." *Kunst für Alle* (Berlin) 25 (1909/10): 465–469.

275. SCHNACK, Anton. "Deutscher Expressionismus, Darmstadt 1920." *Darmstädter Zeitung* (Darmstadt), (24 June 1920).

276. SCHULT, Friedrich, ed. *Ernst Barlach im Gespräch.* Munich: Insel Verlag, 1948.

277. SCHUMANN, Paul. "Ausstellung der Künstlervereinigung Dresden 1916." *Kunst für Alle* (Berlin) 31 (1915/16): 465–474.

278. SECKER, Hans F. "Bemerkungen zu Hans von Marées." *Wallraf-Richartz Jahrbuch* (Cologne) 2 (1925): 164–179.

279. SELZ, Jean. *Modern Sculpture, Origins and Evolution.* New York: Braziller, 1963. p. 147, 161.

280. SERVAES, Franz. "Berliner 'Freie Secession'." *Deutsche Kunst und Dekoration* (Darmstadt) 38 (1916): 157–180.

281. SERVAES, Franz. "Moderne Bildhauer, Sezession, Freie Sezession, Cassirer." *Vossische Zeitung* (Berlin), (27 Apr. 1916).

282. Seuphor, Michel. *La sculpture de ce siècle: Dictionnaire de la sculpture moderne.* Neuchâtel: Editions du Griffon, 1959. p. 47–51.

282a. Seuphor, Michel. *Sculpture of this Century.* New York: Braziller, 1960. English translation of bibl. 282.

282b. Seuphor, Michel. *Die Plastik unseres Jahrhunderts.* Cologne: DuMont-Schauberg, 1959. German translation of bibl. 282.

283. Seymour, Charles. *Tradition and Experiment in Modern Sculpture.* Washington: American University Press, 1949. p. 38–40, ill. p. 39.

284. Soby, James Thrall. "Genesis of a Collection." *Art in America* (New York) 49, no. 1 (1961): 73.

285. Storck, Willi F. "Die Ausstellung des deutschen Künstlerbundes in Mannheim 1913." *Kunst für Alle* (Berlin) 28 (1912/13): 481–493.

286. Storck, Willi F. "Linie und Form, Ausstellung von Zeichnungen und Plastiken neuzeitlicher Bildhauer in der Kunsthalle Mannheim." *Deutsche Kunst und Dekoration* (Darmstadt) 35 (1914/15): 25–40.

287. Sulser, Wilhelm. "Notizen zur Plastiksammlung Werner Bär." *Kunst und Volk* (Zurich) 17 (1955): 77–88.

288. Trier, Eduard. *Moderne Plastik.* Berlin: Gebr. Mann, 1954. p. 30–32.

288a. Trier, Eduard. *Form and Space, Sculpture of the Twentieth Century.* London: Thames and Hudson, 1961. New York, Praeger, 1968. English translation of bibl. 288.

289. Trier, Eduard. *Zeichner des 20. Jahrhunderts.* Berlin: Gebr. Mann, 1956. p. 41–42.

290. Valentiner, Wilhelm R. *Origins of Modern Sculpture.* New York: Wittenborn, 1946.

291. Valentiner, William R. "The Simile in Sculptoral Composition." *The Art Quarterly* (Detroit) 10, no. 4 (1947) 10: 264.

292. Vogeler, Erich. "Die Plastik auf den Berliner Ausstellungen." *Die Plastik* (Munich) 2 (1912): 61–63.

293. Wedderkop, Hermann von. *Deutsche Graphik des Westens.* Weimar: Feuer-Verlag, 1922. p. 10, 37–38, 138–140.

294. Wedderkop, Hermann von. "Grosse Kunstausstellung Duesseldorf." *Der Cicerone* (Leipzig) 12 (1920): 555.

295. Westheim, Paul. " 'Die Schaffenden', Selbstanzeige." *Das Kunstblatt* (Berlin) 2 (1918): 228–229.

296. Westheim, Paul. "Zeitlupe." *Das Kunstblatt* (Berlin) 11 (1927): 306–307.

297. Westheim, Paul. "Zeitlupe." *Das Kunstblatt* (Berlin) 15 (1931): 26.

298. Wild, Doris. "Die Sammlung von Nelly und Werner Bär-Theilheimer." *Das Kunstwerk* (Baden-Baden) 7 (1953): 16–17.

299. Winckelmann, Heinrich, ed. *Der Bergbau in der Kunst.* Essen: Glückauf Verlag, 1958.

300. Woermann, Karl. *Geschichte der Kunst aller Völker und Zeiten.* Vol. 6. *Jüngere Neuzeit von 1750 bis zur Gegenwart.* Leipzig: Bibliographisches Institut, 1922. 2nd ed 1927. p. 441–442.

301. Wolfradt, Willi. "Berliner Ausstellungen." *Der Cicerone* (Leipzig) 16 (1924): 978–979.

302. Wolf, Georg Jacob. "Die Ausstellung der Münchner Neuen Secession." *Kunst für Alle* (Berlin) 36 (1920/21): 347–352.

303. Wolf, Georg Jacob. "Die Internationale Kunstausstellung der Münchner Secession 1911." *Kunst für Alle* (Berlin) 26 (1910/1911). 481–494.

304. Wolf, Georg Jacob. "Münchner Jahresausstellung im Glaspalast, verbunden mit einer Jubiläumsausstellung der Allgemeinen Deutschen Künstlergemeinschaft." *Kunst für Alle* (Berlin) 24 (1908/1909): 561.

305. Wolf, Georg Jacob. "Münchner Sommerausstellungen, Ausstellung der Secession." *Kunst für Alle* (Berlin) 31 (1915/16): 405–433.

306. Wolf, Georg Jacob. "Die Neue Münchner Secession." *Kunst für Alle* (Berlin) 30 (1914/15): 278–280.

307. Zahn, Leopold. "Vom Wechselspiel der Gotik und Klassik in der modernen Kunst." *Feuer* (Weimar) 3 (1920/21): 89.

308. Zeeck, Hans. [Exhibition Review.] *Die Weltkunst* (Munich) 10 (1936): 16.

309. Zoege Von Manteuffel, Karl. "Ausstellung der Freien Secession Berlin." *Kunst für Alle* (Berlin) 29 (1913/14): 465–474.

Who is still here?

Who stayed behind after these murders,

Who survived this bloody sea?

I step across this stubbled field

And look around at the crop

Which murder butchered horribly.

My friends lie all around me,

My brothers are no longer here.

Our faith, love, all is gone,

And Death appears on every path, on every flower.

Damn!

You, who prepared so much death,

Have you no death

      for me?

Wilhelm Lehmbruck, January 1918